Discovering
OCEANS, LAKES, PONDS AND PUDDLES

*Why does it take so much
water to make paper?

*How high can a geyser
shoot into the air?

Discovering
OCEANS, LAKES, PONDS AND PUDDLES

◆ ◆ ◆

Jeron Ashford Frame

Lion Publishing
Oxford ◆ Batavia ◆ Sydney

● ●

Text copyright © 1994 by Jeron Ashford Frame
Illustrations © 1994 by Scott Holladay

Design by Terry Julien

Published by
Lion Publishing
20 Lincoln Avenue, Elgin, IL 60120, USA
ISBN 0 7459 2621 5
Lion Publishing plc
Sandy Lane West, Oxford, England
ISBN 0 7459 2621 5
Albatross Books Pty
PO Box 320, Sutherland, NSW 2232, Australia
ISBN 0 7324 0678 1

First edition 1994

CIP applied for

A catalogue record for this book is available from the British Library

Printed and bound in USA

Contents

"Where can you find water in the desert?

*How can you cool off
on a hot summer day?

*What do you need to make your own igloo?

Chapter 1

The What, When, Where, Why, and How of Water

Water is all around us. We drink it, wash with it, play in it, cook with it, and use it to warm and cool us. Sometimes we can see it, and sometimes we can't. Sometimes it's heavy and hard, and sometimes it's almost as light as air. But whatever form water takes, it's an essential part of our world. In fact, life could not exist on earth without it.

According to the Bible, before there were any plants, animals, and people, the earth was nothing but water. Scientists have many theories about what the earth may have been like then. Some think it was all ice. Others think perhaps it was a big mass of water and water vapour—just as the sun is a ball of fire and gases. Later, when the earth's atmosphere was formed, water in its liquid and solid states stayed on the earth, forming oceans, lakes, glaciers, and ice caps. Water vapour rose into the atmosphere, forming clouds.

But What Is Water?

Like everything else on earth, water is made of molecules. Each molecule is made up of three atoms—two hydrogen atoms and one oxygen atom. Another way of writing it is H_2O. Those three atoms come together to make the streaming, raining, freezing, dripping thing we call water.

Water is one of the most versatile chemical compounds on earth, because it takes so many different forms. It can be a liquid, a solid (ice), or a gas (water vapour or steam). In each of these forms, the water molecule remains the same. But the arrangement of the three atoms in the molecule changes as water freezes or boils.

The temperature at which water boils or freezes is always the same. In fact, scientists based the Celsius temperature scale on the way water reacts to heat and cold: water freezes into ice at 0° Celsius and boils into steam at 100° Celsius.

TRY IT!

Make your own water! Stand a small candle up on a plate and light it. Put a clear glass over it. Once the flame burns up the oxygen, the candle will go out. Now look at the inside of the glass. Where did those water droplets come from?

Wax contains hydrogen. As it melts, the hydrogen joins with the oxygen trapped in the glass and forms water.

Water, Water Everywhere!

Can you think of a living thing that has no water in it at all? Cut open an apple or a carrot, and you can feel the juice on your fingers. That juice is mostly water. If a plant goes without water for several days, it won't be long before it begins to droop and dry up. Play outside on a hot day, and you'll soon get thirsty. All living things need water.

Water Means Life

If you've ever forgotten to water a plant, or seen what lack of rain can do to your garden, you know that plants can't live without a certain amount of water. Plants absorb water from the soil through their roots. The water travels through the stem or trunk to all parts of the plant.

TRY IT!

Get two dry glasses. Put a few spoonfuls of fresh soil in one. Leave the other one empty. Cover both with a dry plate or saucer and leave them overnight. The next day, lift up each saucer and look at the bottom. What did you find? The water droplets on the saucer that covered the dirt came from the soil.

Now try the same experiment with sand. Did you get the same result? Do you think there is water in the desert?

Scientists aren't quite sure exactly how plants draw water up through their stems. But we know it happens.

You can see it happen for yourself. All you need is a white carnation or other light-coloured flower, a glass of water, and some food colouring. Cut the flower's stem at an angle, about 15 cm below the flower's petals. Add a few drops of food colouring to the glass of water, and put the flower stem in the glass. In a few hours the petals will begin to change colour as the water rises up the stem.

Plants not only drink, they also breathe! Plants take in air through tiny openings called stomata on their stems and leaves. During the day, the stomata are open, and water vapour escapes through the openings. When a plant loses more water than it takes in, the water pressure inside it drops, and the plant begins to lose its shape. This is why many plants seem to wilt on a hot summer afternoon.

'Bodies' of Water

Water is the most important element in the bodies of animals and humans. Some creatures contain more water than others. The jellyfish is about 99% water! Human bodies are about 65% water. Sounds impossible, doesn't it? After all, there are a lot of organs and bones and muscle stuffed inside each person. But every single part of the body contains some water.

The average person needs to take in about three litres of water each day. Doctors say we should drink six to eight glasses of water a day—about two litres. That means we need another litre of water from the food we eat. Foods that are especially high in water content are fruit, potatoes, and fish.

If our bodies saved all of that water, we'd probably expand like a water balloon. But most of the water that enters our bodies leaves in our urine. We also lose water vapour when we breathe out.

Lastly, some of the water flows out through the pores in our skin. This is called perspiration. Although we can't see it, our bodies perspire almost all the time—whether we're reading, walking, or sleeping. When heat and exercise speed up perspiration, we can see it on our skin. And that's called sweat! When you are playing sports or riding your bike, your body can lose two litres of water every hour.

Some liquid water is heavier than normal water. One out of every 500 hydrogen atoms is twice as heavy. When it combines with oxygen it forms 'heavy water' What do you think heavy water might be used for? Probably not for taking showers!

One maize plant can lose 900 kg of water during the hot summer months!

Human Being

Water Content:

Brain - 75%
Blood - 83%
Bone - 22%
Kidneys - 83%
Muscle - 75%

If the water our bodies lose is not replaced, we can become dehydrated. The water in our bodies contains salt. Dehydration occurs when a person's salt content or water content—or both—becomes depleted. This usually happens because the person isn't drinking enough water, is vomiting, or has diarrhoea for an extended period of time. A strong thirst, a dry mouth, weight loss, and dry and wrinkly skin are the symptoms of dehydration. To treat it, doctors must replace both the water and the electrolytes, the salt and minerals in the body's water.

It's Not the Heat, It's the Humidity

Perspiring actually helps to keep your body cool in the summer. To understand better how it works, you'll need an electric fan and a steamy room. (To make a steamy room, turn on the hot water in the shower for five minutes and close the door.)

Set up your fan in the kitchen, then run warm water over your hands and arms. Hold them up in front of the fan. Do you feel cooler? Now run warm water over your hands and arms again and go into the steamy room. Which feels cooler—the fan or the steamy room? Chances are, the fan feels cooler.

The sweat on your skin evaporates, or turns into water vapour, when it touches the air. The water vapour leaves your skin and takes some of the heat from your body with it. This cools you off. But air can only hold a certain amount of moisture. When there is a lot of humidity—or water vapour—in the air, the sweat can't turn into water vapour. Because the air in the steamy room was already full of water vapour, there was nowhere for the moisture on your hands and arms to go. When this happens during a humid summer day, perspiration stays on your skin, soaks your clothes, and makes you feel miserable.

Travelling Water

While water vapour always rises, water in its liquid form is heavier than air. So it obeys the laws of gravity just like everything else on earth. Because of gravity, water travels toward the centre of the earth until it is stopped by impenetrable rock. Then it forms oceans, rivers, and lakes.

Liquid water can never travel upward—unless it is pushed or pulled by something stronger than gravity. You've probably proved this hundreds of times with a plain drinking straw. As you suck up some water in a straw, you pull the water up. The next time you're drinking through a straw, try this: suck up some water and quickly cover the top end of the straw with your finger. Lack of air pressure at the top keeps the water in the straw. Remove your finger, and the air pushes the water out of the straw.

With a Little Help from Water

We all know that some things float in water—such as corks and boats. And some things sink—rocks, for example. Flotation has to do with two things called *density* and *water displacement*.

If an object is denser than the water it's put in—say metal or stone—it will sink. If the object is less dense—like plastic or wood—it will float. So how can a huge steel ship float? The answer involves the way metal ships are made and that thing called water displacement.

A ship is made of relatively little steel. Although steel in thin sheets is used to make the hull, the rest of the ship is filled with air pockets—in the cabins, hallways, engine room, and in the hollow hull itself.

When a ship goes into the water, it displaces, or pushes aside, its own weight in water. Because it can push water aside—and because it has lots of air pockets—a ship can float. If the ship were solid steel—without any spaces for air—it would sink.

A submarine uses the principle of air pockets to submerge and surface. To go deep underwater, the crew open valves to let seawater fill large empty tanks in the sub. To surface, the seawater is pumped out of the tanks, and the new air spaces cause the sub to rise to the surface.

Try It!

Fill a sink with water. Place a plastic spoon carefully on the surface of the water. Then place a plastic fork on the water. What happens to the spoon? What happens to the fork?

The spoon floated because its cup shape created an air space and because it was made from a light material. When it floated, it displaced its weight in water. The fork, even though it was less dense than the water, had no air space. It couldn't displace water because of the spaces between its tines. So it sank.

What about a sewing needle? Do you think a needle would float or sink? To find out, fill a cup with water and carefully float a small square of tissue paper on top of the water. Then lay a needle on the paper. Touch the corner of the paper with a pencil to make the paper sink. The needle floats! Now add one drop of washing-up liquid to the water. The needle sinks! What happened?

Actually, when the paper sank away, the needle stayed on top of the water because of surface tension—not because it could float. Surface tension means that water molecules stick together so that objects are able to sit on the water's surface without displacing any water. The washing-up liquid is soapy, and soap doesn't mix well with water. When the soap hit the water's surface, it pushed aside some of the water molecules. The surface tension was broken, and the needle sank.

Surface tension doesn't just help needles to float. It makes raindrops keep their shape. It allows water beetles and pond skaters to walk on top of the water. You can also see surface tension at work when you're painting with watercolours. When you dip the paintbrush in water, the bristles

fan out. But what happens when you pull the paintbrush out? Surface tension causes the bristles to pull together again.

Knotty Water

Amaze your friends by tying water in knots!

You'll need a nail and a plastic or metal container about the size of a catering tin. Use the nail to make three holes in the side of the container, about one to two inches from the bottom. The holes should be 5 mm apart. Hold the container under a running tap until water streams from the three holes. Pinch the three streams together with your fingers and command them, 'Stay!' (The command is optional.) Surface tension should keep the streams together. (If it doesn't work right away, try just two streams at first.) Brush your hand across the streams and they will separate again.

Water, the Super Solvent!

A solvent is a liquid that dissolves other things. You've probably dissolved a lot of things in water: jelly, sugar in tea, and salt in soup.

Over long periods of time, water can even dissolve rock! For example, thousands of years of running water have shaped caves and caverns, mountains, coastlines—even the Grand Canyon in America.

Gasses can also be dissolved in water. We pump air into fish tanks so that the fish can breathe. Carbonated drinks have carbon dioxide dissolved in them. *Alka-Seltzer* tablets contain carbon dioxide that is released when the tablets contact water. The gas produces the 'fizz' when the tablets dissolve. Wouldn't it be great if someone would make soft-drink and juice-flavoured fizzy tablets?

Water can't dissolve everything, but it can dissolve more things than any other liquid.

Chapter 2
Water and the Weather

Most of the comings and goings of water on the earth have to do with the weather.

Through evaporation, water molecules continually rise from the earth in the form of water vapour. The water vapour then turns back into water when it hits the cold air high above the earth. This is called condensation. The water then falls back to the earth in the form of precipitation: rain, snow, sleet, hail, and dew. The whole process is called the water cycle.

Up It Goes . . .

We already know how water evaporates when it's heated in the kettle. Outside, the sun, wind, and air are responsible for evaporation. The sun heats the water and the air dries it on the ground until it turns to vapour.

There It Stays . . .

Air high in the sky is cooler than air near the earth. When water vapour hits cold air, it turns back into liquid. Cold air can't hold as much water vapour as warm air. So some of the vapour condenses into small drops of water. You've seen this happen when drinking a cold glass of pop on a hot day. Little beads of water build up on the outside of the glass. The water forms because water vapour in the air was cooled by the cold glass.

TRY IT!

Fill two glass jars half-full with water. Mark the water level on the outside of both jars. Cover one with aluminium foil. Then set both jars in a warm, sunny place. After a few days, check the water levels. Did both jars lose water? Which jar lost the most? Why do you think one jar didn't lose as much?

Now fill the two jars again to the marks and leave them both uncovered. Put one in the sun and the other in the shade. After a few days, check the water levels. What did you find?

In order for evaporation to take place, the water vapour must rise along with the warm air. The aluminium foil kept the water vapour in the second jar from rising. Dry air makes water evaporate, but the sun makes it evaporate even faster. This is why the jar in the shade didn't evaporate as much.

When small water droplets group together, they form clouds. Clouds can be anywhere, not just in the sky. The steam from a boiling kettle is a cloud. Your breath on a cold day is a cloud. Even the vapour trails from aeroplanes are clouds.

Down It Comes!

Condensed water vapour stays in clouds until it becomes too heavy. Then it falls to earth again. The form it takes—rain, snow, sleet, or hail—depends on the temperature of the air, and the direction and speed of the wind.

Messages in the Sky

The water droplets that make up clouds don't always come together in the same way. There are several different types of clouds, and they all tell us that different things are happening in the atmosphere.

Cumulus clouds are the big, fluffy ones you see on nice summer days.

MAKE YOUR OWN KITCHEN RAINSTORM!

Put a kettle of water on the stove to boil. Fill a pie tin with ice cubes. Hold the tin over the boiling kettle. (Wear a glove so the steam doesn't burn your hand.) The water in the kettle will evaporate, forming clouds of water vapour that rise up to the pie tin. As the water vapour hits the cold pie tin, it will condense and form water droplets on the tin. What happens when the drops get bigger?

TRY IT!

Make a cloud chart. Keep track for a week of the types of clouds you see each day. You'll probably need to check the sky two or three times a day. Can you predict when a storm is coming?

You can find the most interesting cloud pictures in cumulus clouds.

Cumulo-nimbus clouds, sometimes called thunderheads, occur when cumulus clouds rise high in the sky. They are dark, threatening-looking clouds. When you see these coming, you can be pretty sure a thunderstorm is on the way.

Cirrus clouds are thin and wispy and are found high in the sky on dry days. They are so high that they are made entirely of ice crystals. Cirrus clouds may look pretty. But they usually mean there's a 'front' on the way. A front is when cold and warm air push against each other. Fronts bring a change of weather—and sometimes rain or snow.

When a front moves in, clouds form a little lower in the sky. *Stratus* clouds are layered and frequently cover the whole sky. They are responsible for grey, overcast days.

Nimbo-stratus clouds are often dark and bring continuous rain or snow. You can see the many layers with different shades of grey.

Wet Air

You've probably heard people in the summer complain, 'It's not the heat, it's the humidity.' Humidity is the amount of water vapour in the air around us. Weather reporters measure humidity in percentages. The

amount of humidity in the air can make the temperature feel warmer or colder than it actually is.

Eighty percent humidity means the air is 80% water vapour. On an especially warm day, 80% humidity feels muggy, sticky, and uncomfortable. A dry, more comfortable day might have 30% humidity.

High humidity levels usually occur in warmer weather. But humidity varies with climate. Some places are more humid than others no matter what the temperature or season.

Rain, Rain, Don't Go Away!

The tiny droplets in the clouds soon join each other to make bigger and bigger drops. If the air in the upper atmosphere is rising, it pushes more and more drops together. Soon the drops become too heavy for the air to hold up. Then some of that water has to come down.

Raindrops come in all sizes. When rain falls in tiny droplets, we call it drizzle. On the other hand, sometimes it's 'raining cats and dogs'. Those big raindrops may not really be as big as animals, but they can make you soaking wet in no time! Can you think of some other fun expressions about rain?

TRY IT!

Measure the amount of rainfall in your area with your own rain gauge. You'll need a clear plastic lemonade bottle. Take off the coloured bottom cup, if there is one. Then cut the top off the bottle and put it upside down into the rest of the bottle to make a funnel. Put a piece of masking tape on the side of the bottle. Use a ruler to mark centimetres on the tape, starting at the bottom of the bottle.

Set up your rain gauge in your garden, in an open area, sheltered from the wind. Check the amount of rain that falls each rainy day, and compare your findings with those of the local weather centre.

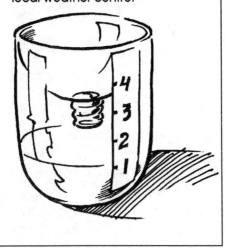

Weather Forecasting

Rain has always played a big part in the lives and livelihoods of human beings. For people who depend on their crops for food, too much or too little rain can mean starvation during the coming winter. A sudden storm can mean tragedy for a sailor at sea.

Over the centuries, people have found interesting ways to predict rain. They have discovered that the sky, the earth, animals, and even their own bodies can help them tell when a storm is on the way.

One of the best-known rain proverbs is, 'Red sky at night, shepherd's delight. Red sky in the morning, shepherd take warning.' This idea is even in the Bible: 'When evening comes, you say, "It will be fair weather, for the sky is red," and in the morning, "Today it will be stormy, for the sky is red and overcast."' Here's how it works. A red sunrise means there's a lot of water vapour in the air, which means high humidity. And often high humidity means rain is on the way.

Many other rain proverbs are true too. But some simply developed from rumours and stories, and they are not accurate at all. Here are a few common rain proverbs that all have at least a little truth in them.

The further away things look, the nearer the rain.

Swallows fly low before rain.

Rain before seven, clear by eleven.

Sound travelling far and wide, a stormy day this does betide.

When the hair on the scalp turns limp, it will rain on the morrow.

Here's why these sayings can help you predict rain:

Low atmospheric pressure means a storm is coming, and low pressure means faraway objects look clearer.

Low pressure interferes with a bird's flying, so birds fly closer to the ground when a storm is coming.

Most normal storm fronts take about four hours to pass through.

Sound waves can't travel as far when air pressure is low and humidity is high, so sounds are 'blocked' and they seem louder.

Human hair, especially blonde hair, soaks up moisture from the air and goes limp. In fact, scientists use blonde hair in hygrometers, instuments which measure humidity.

Many cultures that depend on rain and snow for drinking water and irrigation have developed ways to 'make' rain. Native Americans believed that a ceremonial rain dance would please the gods and bring rain. Today scientists can actually make rain and snow by cloud seeding. To 'seed' a cloud, aeroplanes fly above the clouds and drop either granules of dry ice or a chemical called silver iodide into the clouds. Ice crystals form around the tiny bits of ice and chemicals. Then, depending on the air temperature, raindrops or snowflakes soon begin to fall.

Let It Snow, Let It Snow, Let It Snow

When the air inside a cloud is very cold, the water droplets there will freeze. As they freeze, thousands of them attach themselves to a speck of

The most snow to fall in one day in the U. S. A., 376 cm, was at Silver Lake, Colorado, in April 1921. Mt. Shasta, California, holds the record for the most snow in one storm: 480 cm, 13-19 February 1959.

dust or ice and become a snowflake. The shape of a snowflake depends on the height and temperature of the clouds, how much moisture is present, how fast they fall, and what kind of weather they fall through.

What Colour Is Snow?

Of course, everyone knows that snow is white. . . . Don't they? Actually, snowflakes are clear. They only look white because of the way they reflect light. But would you believe that in some areas of the western United States and Canada, snow can be pink or blue or green!

Pink snow is caused by particles of red soil that are carried into the air. Snowflakes form around the particles and look pink. Other snow-flakes can form around tiny plants, called cryoplankton, that live in the atmosphere. These plants can make snow look many different colours.

Try It!

Are there really no two snowflakes alike? See for yourself. The next time the forecast predicts snow, put a sheet of black sugar paper in the freezer. When the snow begins to fall, take the paper and a magnifying glass outside. Catch a few snowflakes on the paper and look at them under the magnifying glass. Any similarities? (Note, though, that all snowflakes have one thing in common: six sides.)

Wet Snow/Dry Snow

Even though all snow is frozen water, it isn't all the same. One way to see snow's differences is to melt it. Usually, ten centimetres of snow will melt into one centimetre of water. But that isn't always true. The amount of water depends on whether you're melting dry snow or wet snow.

Dry snow is made from flakes that form in areas far from the oceans and seas. Once it falls, it blows around and is impossible to press into a snowball. Dry snow is great for skiers—who sometimes call it 'powder'—because it doesn't melt quickly and stick to their skis.

Wet snow falls in areas near the ocean and other large bodies of water. Wet snow packs hard and makes great snowpeople and snow forts. It is much heavier than dry snow, and can be exhausting to shovel. If you tried to catch and observe snowflakes on a sheet of black paper and it didn't work, chances are the snow was too wet. Instead of sticking, the separate flakes probably just melted together.

The people who live in arctic areas know all about these different kinds of snow. The Inuit, or Eskimo people, have dozens of names for snow. The all-purpose word is *annui*. Windblown snow is *upsik*. Fluffy snow is *theh-ni-zee*. They also have words for falling snow, packed snow, snow where reindeer graze, and snow that is good for igloos.

Look Out Below!

Snowflakes are beautiful and almost as light as air. But snow in large amounts can be dangerous—especially when it collects on steep hills and mountains.

When fresh, powdery snow falls on top of old layers of snow and ice, it can't stick. A strong wind or sudden rain can cause the entire mass of

snow to slide. This is called an avalanche. Loose snow avalanches start with a small amount of snow and pick up more and more on the way down. In a slab avalanche, a large chunk of snow breaks off and slides in one big heap.

Some avalanches can slide at up to 24 kilometres per hour, burying trees, houses, and any people that happen to be in the way. That doesn't seem very fast, unless you're standing at the bottom!

Many people believe a loud noise can start an avalanche, but there is little evidence for this belief.

This Is Slick! (And Not So Slick)

Often snow will melt and then quickly freeze again, forming a layer of ice on streets and sidewalks that can cause a lot of problems for cars, trains, and pedestrians. Sometimes rain freezes as it falls, building up on trees, windscreens, and aeroplane wings. Its weight can pull down branches of trees and collapse roofs.

In cities and towns, salt—and sometimes sand—is routinely spread on roads to melt winter ice. But salting roads has its drawbacks. Salt water can damage roads and kill plants and trees. When it seeps into streams and ponds, it can cause some types of algae to grow uncontrollably. Sometimes birds and small animals have died from drinking salty melted snow. In the same way, sand on the roads can be a nuisance when it blows around and clogs up storm sewers.

Try It!

A common way to get rid of ice is to sprinkle salt on it. To see how this works up close, lay a toothpick or a used match on top of an ice cube. Sprinkle salt around the toothpick. Wait a few minutes, then lift the toothpick. It should be frozen to the ice cube.

The salt melted the ice around the toothpick. This is because salt water must be colder than 0° Celsius to freeze. The area under the toothpick didn't have salt on it, so the toothpick froze to the cube.

Golf Balls from the Sky

Hail is one of the most damaging kinds of precipitation. Hailstones form when there are strong upward air currents inside a cumulo-nimbus cloud. The falling ice crystals are blown back up and more ice forms around them. Air currents keep blowing the crystals back up until they are so heavy they fall to the ground as hard balls of snow and ice.

The next time it hails, try cutting open a hailstone. You should be able to see the layers of ice. Count them to find out how many times that hailstone was blown back up into the cloud.

Dew, Frost, and Fog: Weather on the Ground

Precipitation doesn't always come from the sky. On spring and autumn mornings, you may find that the grass is covered with dew. The ground absorbs heat during the day and radiates out some of that heat at night. At the same time, the air near the ground cools. When the air is calm and filled with enough water vapour, some of that vapour will condense on the ground. Droplets form on the grass, plants, and the

bicycle that you left outside last night.

If the temperature reaches freezing point, the dew will freeze into ice crystals and become frost. This happens more often on clear nights. On cloudy nights, the heat radiating from the earth is pushed down by the clouds and the temperature near the earth stays warmer. When weather forecasters issue a frost warning, it's a good idea to cover any early plants. Frost will kill most spring and summer plants.

Fog develops when there is a high concentration of dust or pollen, as well as water vapour, in the air. The water vapour condenses around the dust or pollen particles, forming what look like clouds along the ground. Fog also occurs near large bodies of water, where cool air and warm air often meet and form clouds.

Chapter 3
Oceans and Seas

About 70% of the earth's surface is covered by oceans, and ocean water accounts for most of the water on our planet. Yet the ocean is one of the places on earth that we have explored the least. Its wonders—and its mysteries—may never be completely understood by human beings.

The Making of an Ocean

When God created dry land, the oceans first took form. Scientists have discovered that the ocean floor, which is the thinnest part of the earth's crust, is in some places either pulling apart or pushing together. From this discovery came the idea that all dry land used to be just one big continent. The theory is that, over time, the land pulled apart and drifted into the seven large continents we have now. These shifting continents then divided the huge body of water into the four oceans: the Atlantic, the Pacific, the Indian, and the Arctic.

The largest and deepest ocean is the Pacific. It contains nearly 50% of all the water on earth. It also covers more area than all the land on earth put together. If you have a globe, you can see this for yourself. Turn it so you are facing the centre of the Pacific Ocean. How much land can you see? If you were looking at this view of Earth from space, the whole planet would look blue.

The Ocean's Layers

The temperature of the ocean varies with the depth and the surrounding air pressure. At the North and South Poles, for example, the surface

DISCOVER A NEW OCEAN!

If you look at a new globe or map of the world, you may find a new ocean—the Southern Ocean. It circles around the entire globe, at the edges of Antarctica. Scientists claim that the Southern Ocean deserves its own name because it's colder and has much stronger currents than the Atlantic and Pacific oceans that flow into it.

water reaches only -2° Celsius. Near the equator, the sun warms the surface waters to about 30° Celsius or more. But even on the hottest days the sun can only warm the top few hundred metres of water. The deeper parts of the ocean, which may receive little or no light, average about 3° Celsius.

The top 200 metres of the ocean is called the *sunlit zone*. The next 1000 metres, called the *twilight zone*, receives only a little sunlight. The deepest part of the ocean, down to about 7000 metres, is called the *dark zone*. Because each zone receives varying amounts of sunlight, different plants and sea animals live in each zone.

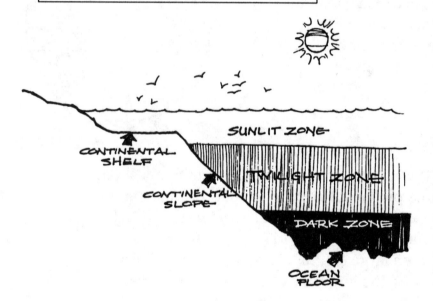

The Ocean Floor

Walking into the ocean is like walking into the deep end of a swimming pool. The ground slopes down further and further. The shallow area near the shore is called the continental shelf. Further on, the land plunges steeply down to the ocean floor. This is called the continental slope.

From this point on, the ocean is nothing like a swimming pool! Mountain ranges rise up from the floor. Some mountains break through the surface to form islands and volcanoes. Caves and crevices dot the landscape, while canyons and deep valleys, called trenches, plunge thousands of metres deeper than the rest of the ocean floor.

TOO DEEP FOR ME!

The average depth of the ocean is about 4,500 metres. However, the Marianas Trench in the Pacific Ocean is 12,000 metres deep.

Look! Sea!

Even though people use the words *ocean* and *sea* interchangeably, a sea is really a smaller section of an ocean. Most seas border the land and are fed by rivers. Some bodies of water that are completely surrounded by land may be called seas—such as the Dead Sea in the Middle East—but they are really saltwater lakes.

Some of the more familiar seas known around the world include:

• *the Mediterranean Sea*, which lies between Europe, Asia, and Africa

• *the North Sea*, between Great Britain and Denmark

• *the Caribbean Sea*, bordered by Central America, South America, and the West Indies

DID YOU KNOW?

The Sargasso Sea lies right in the middle of the Atlantic Ocean, between North America and Africa. It's a calm area, with no currents and very little wind. It gets its name from the masses of sargassum seaweed floating on the surface. For centuries sailors avoided the Sargasso Sea because they feared their ships would get tangled in the seaweed and sink.

• *the Red Sea*, in North-east Africa, which the Bible says God once divided, allowing the prophet Moses and his followers to walk across on dry land as they escaped slavery in Egypt.

Salty Water

If you've ever gone swimming in the ocean, probably one of the first things you noticed about the water was its taste. In general, there are about 30 ml of salt in each litre of sea water. The oceans are salty because the rivers that flow into them carry minerals and salts from the land. Over millions of years these ingredients have collected in the oceans, making the water salty.

An Egg That Treads Water

Besides its salt content, how is salt water different from fresh water? See for yourself!

Get two large jars and fill them both about two-thirds full with water.

Add four tablespoons of table salt to one of the jars. Stir it until it dissolves. Now get two uncooked eggs. Carefully put an egg in each jar. What happens to the eggs?

Salt dissolved in water increases the water's density, or thickness. Things that would normally sink, such as eggs, can float in water that is more dense. If you've ever been swimming in the ocean, you probably found it easier to float than in a swimming pool.

Ocean water is, of course, too salty to drink. But some countries that don't have enough fresh water have learned to make ocean water fit for human use. The process, called *desalination,* involves heating salt water until it evaporates, leaving the salt behind. Then the water vapour is transported over pipes containing cold water. When the hot vapour meets the cold water, it condenses back into water, this time without the salt. Kuwait and Saudi Arabia use desalted water. Unfortunately, desalination is expensive. The countries that are most in need of fresh water, particularly for irrigating their crops, can't afford it.

Now try your own desalination experiment. First, pour the salty water—minus the egg—into a pan and heat it on the stove. After it boils, turn the heat down and put a lid on the pan. Every two or three minutes, carefully lift the lid and pour the water that has condensed on it into a cup. (Use an oven glove or potholder so you don't get burned by the steam.) Replace the pan lid so more water can condense. When you have enough water in the cup to taste—and it's cool enough to drink— take a sip. Is it still salty?

Try It!

You don't have to live by the sea to make and enjoy salt water toffee. Ask a grown-up to help you.

Mix together and stir over low heat until dissolved:

30

450 g sugar
12 fl oz water
8 fl oz glucose syrup
7.5 ml salt
10 ml glycerine

Bring gently to the boil, stir and cover. Cook for about 3 minutes. Then uncover and cook without stirring until it reaches 135°C/265°F on a sugar thermometer. Remove from heat and add 50 mg margarine.

Rub margarine over a large baking tray. Holding the pan away from you, pour the hot syrup slowly onto the tray. While it's cooling a few minutes, drizzle on food colouring and/or flavouring if you like. (Try peppermint or vanilla to start.) Then, using a heat-proof spatula, start scooping up the syrup around the edges and pushing it to the middle. Do this until the mixture is cool enough to touch with your fingers. Then pick up one end of the toffee, pull it up about 40 cm, and fold it back down. If you're working with a friend, you can each hold an end and work the toffee as if you're folding a blanket. Keep this up until the toffee becomes opaque, shiny, and elastic—anywhere from 5 to 20 minutes.

Spread icing sugar on the worktop or large tray, or on nonstick baking paper. Roll the toffee into a large ball and start pulling it at one end until it forms a long rope. Lay the rope in the icing

sugar, cut it up into bite-size pieces, and let it cool. After the toffee cools, wrap the pieces individually in wax paper or place them in an airtight container so they don't dry out and get hard.

Oceans on the Move

The ocean is always moving, even on the calmest days. On the ocean surface, waves ripple along, getting bigger and bigger until they break near the shore. At the same time, just under the surface and deep in the ocean, currents keep the water moving continually in the same direction. And each day the level of the ocean rises at high tide and falls at low tide.

Waves

The surface waters of the ocean move in waves. The size of a wave depends on how strong the wind is blowing. The stronger the wind, the larger and farther apart the waves get.

Even though waves travel across the ocean surface, the water actually stays in the same place. In a wave, the water just moves around in a circle, up and down. The high point of the wave is called the crest. The low point is called the trough. Objects travelling on the ocean are tossed from wave to wave. Closer to the shore, the circles flatten out and the waves get higher. Soon the tops of the waves rise so steeply that they 'break', or fall over.

Water on the Attack

On 1 April 1946, people who lived on the beaches of Hawaii awoke to silence. For the first time ever, no waves splashed on the shore. Little did the people know that more than 3,000 km away, near Alaska, an earthquake had occurred in one of the ocean's deep trenches. They could not know that in just a few minutes all the water that the earthquake had pulled away from their shores would come crashing down on them in waves 8 metres high! The earthquake-caused waves, called a tsunami, travelled at about 450 km per hour and took only five hours to reach the Hawaiian Islands.

Currents

A current is like a river within the ocean that flows in the same direction all the time. Currents flow at all levels of the ocean. Surface currents can be caused by the wind and by the rotation of the earth. Deep currents are caused by differences in temperature and water density (saltiness). If there were no currents at all, oceans would just sit there and become stagnant.

When warm water flows into an ocean, it eventually rises above the colder water. The temperature of ocean water is constantly changing, so warm water and less salty water are always rising. This constant movement keeps a current going.

TRY IT!

Find out what happens when cold water meets warm water. You'll need two empty, clean bottles (old jars of equal size would be fine), a few index cards, and a large plastic container.

Fill one jar with cold water and the other with very warm water. Put a drop of food colouring in the warm water jar. Stand the warm water jar in the container. Put an index card on top of the cold water jar and, keeping the card in place, carefully turn the jar over. (Hold it over the container!)

Air pressure should keep the card in place and the water in the jar. Now put the upside-down cold water jar on top of the warm water jar, and slide away the card. What happens?

Warm water is lighter, or less dense, than cold water. This is why it rose into the cold water.

The most famous current is the Gulf Stream. It flows from the Gulf of Mexico to northern Europe. Travelling by ship from America to Europe is like riding your bike with the wind at your back. The Gulf Stream helps carry the ships. The Gulf Stream also brings warm water to the European coast. Without it, the weather in northern Europe would be much colder.

Ebb and Flow

Once or twice a day the level of the ocean rises and falls. These movements are called tides. If you are on the beach at low tide, you can see that the water's edge is further away. At high tide, the water comes higher up on the beach.

Tides are caused by the gravitational pull of the moon and, to a lesser degree, the sun. Ocean water is pulled away from the earth by the gravity of the sun and moon. And as the earth rotates, the moon and sun pull different ocean areas.

The moon also affects how high and how low the water gets at each tide. When the moon and sun are aligned and pull from the same direction, high tides are very high and low tides are very low. These are called *spring tides*. Spring tides usually happen twice a month, during full moons and new moons. During *neap tides*, the difference between high tide and low tide is much smaller. Neap tides occur when the moon is partially visible. The sun and moon are not aligned, so the gravitational pull is not as strong.

DID YOU KNOW?

Many harbours must have locking gates to keep the water in so that ships in the harbour don't get stranded on dry land when the tide goes out.

Creatures of the Sea

Jellyfish, angelfish, starfish, blowfish . . . there are thousands of different kinds of sea creatures, and they aren't all fish! Each zone of the ocean provides different amounts of light and different kinds of food. So the creatures of the ocean have adapted to the zone that suits them best.

Life Near the Shore

If you check out your family's or friends' seashell collections, you'll probably see a lot of the same kind of shells and ocean creatures. Most of the creatures that are washed ashore by the tides live in the shallow water over the continental shelf. Mussels, cockles, and starfish are pretty easy to identify. Crabs, lobsters, and shrimps are easy to catch in shallow-water fishing nets and traps.

Many shallow water ocean creatures can be observed easily in rock or tidal pools. A tidal pool forms when tides rise and fill up low spots on the shore. The animals that wash in with the tide must adapt to life in the shallow pool as well as in the ocean. Animals with shells, such as mussels, can shut up tight during low tide. Other sea creatures, such as sand worms, burrow into the sand and wait until the next high tide.

Life in a tidal pool can be pretty rough, especially with waves crashing around all the time. Most shallow water animals, such as mussels, starfish, and sea anemones, have shells or spiny coverings to protect them. And many animals and plants have special suction cup 'feet' that they use to cling to rocks when the waves get rough.

Shallow ocean waters are the place to go if you want to fish. These areas are filled with plankton, which are microscopic plants and animals. The smaller species of fish, such as herring and mackerel, travel around the shallow water feeding on plankton. Larger fish, such as tuna, then eat the herring and mackerel. That is, if they aren't caught by fishing boats first!

Sea Plants

When you're wading on the seashore, it's hard not to get tangled up with seaweed! Seaweed is the most visible ocean plant, but it actually accounts for only 1% of ocean plant life. The other 99% is phytoplank-

SEAWEED IN THE FREEZER

Many shallow-water creatures feed only on certain types of seaweed. Seaweeds have flexible leaves and strong stems to keep them from being ripped apart by the waves.

People use seaweed for all kinds of things—building materials, dyes, even medicines. Check out the list of ingredients on the carton of ice cream in your freezer. Do you see *carrageen*? Carrageen is a seaweed that makes ice cream shiny and smooth.

ton—microscopic plants that can grow so quickly and thickly near the shore that they sometimes turn the water a murky green or red. Many species of fish live solely on phytoplankton. In cool, shallow water, phytoplankton can reproduce so quickly the fish don't even have to look for food. They just open their mouths and swim!

The cold waters of the Pacific Ocean are home to forests—but not forests of trees. Giant kelp, a type of seaweed, can grow to 30 metres high. Kelp plants anchor themselves to rocks on the ocean floor and keep growing as long as they get sunlight. Small bulbs filled with gas keep the tops of the kelp floating on the water's surface.

Life in the Sunlit Zone

You may have seen a jellyfish floating on the top of the ocean. Did you know that jellyfish never submerge? They are one of many sea creatures that spend their lives floating. The Portuguese man-of-war is one of the most beautiful floaters—and one of the most dangerous. It has long tentacles drifting below the surface that catch and poison even

DID YOU KNOW?

Many ocean creatures that look like plants are actually animals. The most colourful animals-in-disguise live in coral reefs, which are underwater hills built by tree-shaped animals called coral. Sea fans, anemones, sponges, sea urchins, and barnacles cling to the surface of the reef. And because these plant-like animals are so colourful, many of the most colourful species of fish try to camouflage themselves in coral reefs.

large fish. The giant sea turtle is another creature that stays at the top. The only time sea turtles leave the ocean is to lay their eggs on the shore.

Thousands of species of fish live in the sunlit zone. But they all fall into one of two categories: those with bony skeletons and those with skeletons of cartilage. If you've ever got a fish bone in your mouth, you know what a bony skeleton is! Most small and medium-sized fish have bony skeletons. These fish have bladders filled with air inside their bodies to help them float.

Sharks, skates, and rays have skeletons made of soft cartilage. Because they don't have air bladders, these fish must swim constantly or rest on the ocean floor. There are more than 19,000 species of bony fish and about 600 species of cartilaginous fish.

Fishy Facts

Have you ever noticed when eating fish that the edges are sometimes sticky? Fish secrete mucus through their skin. The mucus helps a fish swim fast and protects it against parasites. Other special body parts fish have that you already know about are gills. Gills contain many tiny blood vessels that carry oxygen into the fish's bloodstream. As water enters the fish's mouth, it passes over the gills. The gills absorb oxygen from the water and release carbon dioxide, allowing the fish to breathe underwater.

All fish have fins and tails, and most of them use their fins and tails to swim and steer. But not every fish swims the same way. Some use their fins to balance. Others swim by sculling, wiggling their bodies back and forth. A tuna, for instance, uses only its powerful tail to swim, because its body is rigid.

Most fish are carnivorous, eating other fish and sea animals. Zooplankton is the most common fish food. It's made up of fish eggs, larvae, and microscopic animals. Where zooplankton is thick, you'll probably find large schools of small fish, such as herring. Believe it or not, the largest fish in the world, the whale shark, eats the smallest food! Whale sharks survive on a diet of phytoplankton and small fish, such as sardines.

Be a Fish Detective

Fish scales grow throughout a fish's entire life. The next time your parents plan to buy fish, ask them to get a whole one that hasn't been skinned. Remove one of the scales with a pair of tweezers and examine it under a magnifying glass or microscope. Can you see rings on the scale? A fish scale grows just like a tree, adding a ring each year or so. If you count the rings, you can tell about how old the fish was.

Life in the Twilight and Dark Zones

The creatures that live in the murky twilight and dark zones are some of the most interesting in the world. They live in depths between 27 metres and 7,000 metres—and some even deeper, down in the trenches of the sea. No plants can grow at these depths, so twilight and dark zone creatures must hang around waiting for food to drift down to them from above. Many deep zone creatures also are scavengers: they wait for dead fish to sink down to them, and then they eat the carcasses.

Twilight zone creatures are usually darker in colour so they can blend in with their dark surroundings. Many of them have their own built-in 'flashlights' that are actually used for camouflage. When the larger, fish-eating animals of the deep zone look up, they see these twilight zone creatures as dark shapes against a lighter blue background. So the lights help the creatures blend in.

TRY IT!

Most zoos and wildlife parks have fish in their displays. The fish are kept in special tanks that are lit dimly or with ultra-violet light. Plan a family trip to an aquarium near you.

The anglerfish uses his flashlight in a different way. This fish has a little 'lightbulb' that dangles over his mouth. He waves it around and lures smaller fish toward his mouth. When the small fish gets close enough—CHOMP!

In the depths of the dark zone, it's hard to find food and mates. Most dark zone fish, such as viperfish and swallowers, have huge mouths—with long, sharp teeth—and expandable stomachs. They can eat fish larger than themselves and then lie on the ocean floor for days while their meal digests. Other dark zone creatures, such as the tripod fish, have legs instead of fins. They walk along the ocean floor and scoop up food that has fallen from the waters above.

Giant Creatures of the Deep

The shark in *Jaws*, Pinocchio riding in the whale, an intelligent dolphin named Flipper . . . are they fact or fiction? Sharks and sea mammals have been the subjects of stories and legends for centuries, probably because they are the biggest of the ocean animals. But what's true?

People believe all sorts of terrible things about sharks. But despite their bad reputation, most sharks are beautiful, mysterious creatures that rarely attack people. In fact, the biggest shark of all is actually harmless. The whale shark grows to more than 18 metres in length, but it has no teeth and eats only plankton. The most dangerous shark, though, is the great white shark, which grows to 5-7 metres. It has razor-sharp, jagged teeth that are at least 7 cm long. A great white shark can easily sense motion and blood in the water and can quickly home in on the source.

You probably already know that whales are not true fish—they're mammals. They need to surface to breathe air and they nurse their young. Dolphins and porpoises are among the smallest and most intelli-

gent whales. The largest whale is the blue whale. It grows to 33 metres long and can weigh more than 150 tonnes. Scientists believe that the blue whale is the largest animal ever to have lived.

Will the Legendary Creatures Live On?

Most marine mammals have thick layers of blubber, strong and durable skins, and beautiful fur—all very useful materials for human beings. The Eskimos, for example, have hunted sea mammals for centuries, using blubber oil for candles and lamps; fur and skins for clothing, tents, and cooking utensils; bones for tools; and nearly every part for food.

Unfortunately, many larger nations haven't used sea mammals so wisely.

When people came from Europe to North America, whaling became a major industry. By the early 1900s, whales were in danger of becoming extinct. Then in 1946 the International Whaling Commission was established to set limits on how many and what kinds of whales countries are allowed to catch. Scientists estimate that before whaling became popular, there were over 200,000 whales in the world. Now there are only about 1,000.

The Lost City Under the Sea

The deep parts of the ocean have been a mystery to humans for centuries. Only in the last few decades have submarines and deep sea divers been able to explore the oceans. Long before exploration began, though, people who lived near the oceans created legends about the sea. One of those legends is about a city called Atlantis.

More than 2,000 years ago, a Greek philosopher named Plato wrote two stories about Atlantis. He said that Atlantis was a large island west of Greece that had disappeared into the sea after a flood. Plato said Atlantis had been a great, wealthy nation with a strong army and a strong government. Most people think Plato made the story up. But others believe there really could have been another continent in the Atlantic Ocean.

Ever since Plato wrote his stories, these people have been searching for Atlantis and making up even more legends about it. For example, some explorers think Atlantis may be in the Bermuda Triangle, an area near the Caribbean Sea where several ships and planes have supposedly disappeared mysteriously.

People Under the Sea

Many, many stories have been told about people who live in the sea—people who are half-human and half-fish. In some legends from sea countries around the world, these merfolk (*mer* is the French word for 'sea') are dangerous and try to lure landpeople to their deaths in the ocean. In other stories, such as Hans Christian Andersen's *The Little Mermaid*, they are a lot like ordinary human beings.

The Story of the Silly Mermaid

Once there was a mermaid who was very silly and very spoiled. When she fell in love with a whale named Long John, she chased him all over the bay and tried in vain to get him to marry her. (Now Long John was a kind whale, but he didn't want any part of this silly mermaid's ridiculous schemes.)

The mermaid didn't take kindly to refusals. So she swam off to her father and demanded angrily, 'I want Long John to be my husband! Make him marry me.'

'My daughter, don't be a fool,' said her father. 'Merfolk do not marry whales.'

But the mermaid would not give up. And, in a short while, she had come up with a plan. 'If I could just get on Long John's back,' she thought, 'I could bridle him and make him do whatever I want.' So she tried tempting Long John with seaweed cakes. She sang loudly to him day and night. But whenever she got close, Long John spouted and dived to the bottom of the sea.

There was only one person Long John feared, and that was Ichabod the whale hunter, who had been trying to catch him for years. At last the mermaid gathered up all her jewels and presented them to Ichabod. 'These are yours,' she told him, 'if you will capture Long John for me.'

Ichabod stroked his chin thoughtfully. 'I have no use for jewels,' he said. 'But if you stop all of that horrible singing day and night, I'll make a deal with you. Tell Long John that if he will let you bridle him and ride him once around the bay, I'll never harpoon him.'

The mermaid shrieked with glee and rushed off to deliver the message.

Long John was a wise old whale. He knew that once the mermaid had him bridled, once around the bay would never be enough for her. Still, to be free forever from Ichabod's dreaded harpoon would be a wonderful thing indeed.

'Very well,' said Long John, and he let the mermaid put her bridle over his head. Up she climbed onto his back, and off they sailed along the coast. The mermaid, certain that she had won Long John as her husband, waved proudly and triumphantly to everyone she met.

As they passed the lighthouse on the point, Ichabod raised his hand to his brow and gave Long John a big grin. Long John winked back at him, then he dived under the surface and quickly rose up again. Before the mermaid could think, Long John spouted her high into the air.

The silly mermaid flew over the sea, over the shore, and over the mountains. She landed with a loud splash in a distant lake, far from home.

Long John lived a safe and happy life in the bay. And the last anyone heard of the mermaid, she was trying to avoid the affections of a lake trout who was even sillier than she was!

Chapter 4
Rivers and Lakes

What do you think would happen to your city or town if it stopped raining forever? The ground would dry up. Lakes, rivers, and ponds would evaporate and disappear. Grass, plants, and trees would die. Animals and people would begin to die. And, maybe far away from your town, the oceans would gradually get smaller. That's how important fresh water is to the earth.

It Starts with a Trickle. . .

Many rivers begin as melting snow and ice high in the mountains. Other rivers begin with rain. Rain soaks into the ground until it reaches a bed of hard rock. Pulled by gravity, it runs along the rock, looking for a way out. When the water finally finds an opening, it flows out of the ground as a spring.

These little trickles flow downhill and become streams. The streams merge to form larger streams called tributaries. Falling rain adds more water to the streams. By the time the streams reach more level land, they form a fully fledged river.

Rub, Rub, Rub

When water flows constantly over one place, the topsoil and loose rocks are washed away, and the ground is worn down. If the water is flowing very fast or if the ground is soft, the river bed becomes deeper and deeper.

DID YOU KNOW?

The River Nile, which flows from central Africa north to the Mediterranean Sea, is the longest river in the world: 6,670 km long! Second longest is the Amazon, which flows from west to east across South America. The third longest river is the Mississippi, which flows from north to south through the United States.

Given enough time, a fast-flowing river can erode deep pathways in the earth. These are called ravines or gorges. The largest gorge caused by a river is the Grand Canyon in America.

When rivers begin in the mountains, they flow very fast. Large rocks and boulders can break off and be swept away in the current. The rocks bump against each other and against the ground, breaking off even more rock and soil.

Eventually a river slows down when the land flattens out. When the water flows more slowly, it can't break off as much rock or carry as much eroded material. Then the heavier gravel and sand sink to the river bottom, and the water becomes brown or yellow with mud.

Water Falls

In the mountains and rocky hills, a river sometimes flows down steep slopes or from high ground to low ground, creating a natural waterfall. Victoria Falls on the Zambezi River in Africa is a good example. It falls over 100 metres from a high plateau to a flat plain.

Waterfalls can also form in more level areas where a river flows more slowly. Here's how it happens.

As it travels, a river passes over many different kinds of rock. Some, such as

DO-IT-YOURSELF EROSION

Scoop up a hill of earth outside. Slowly pour a glass of water on the top of the hill. Notice how the water washes away little channels as it flows down. The water is actually lifting the loose particles of dirt and carrying them down. Those particles help push others out of the way, until they all pile up at the bottom.

45

HOW OLD DID YOU SAY?

Geologists estimate that it takes 30,000 years for the earth's surface to erode one metre. The Grand Canyon, which is 6-30 km wide and up to 1 mile deep, took millions of years to form.

granite, are hard. Other rock is soft, such as limestone and chalk. When hard and soft rocks are layered in the earth, they will erode unevenly.

When water passes over them, the softer layers of rock underneath will slowly be washed away, forming a ledge. As more and more soft rock erodes, the ledge gets bigger. The more erosion that takes place, the higher and steeper the waterfall.

The Journey of a River

Every river is different, but most rivers run in fairly predictable patterns. Have you ever seen a river from an aeroplane? You probably noticed that the river itself is lower than the land on either side of it. In other words, the river forms a valley. If the valley is deep, we know that the river eroded mostly downward. If the valley is flat and wide, we know that the river eroded mostly from side to side.

A FALLING ANGEL?

The highest waterfall in the world is Angel Falls in Venezuela. It measures about 1,000 metres from top to bottom!

Even the straightest-flowing rivers have a few bends and curves. When rivers flow, they don't erode the river bed evenly. Some parts of the river bed get worn away and other parts get built up with rocks and sand. Soon these parts become 'islands.' The river starts flowing around the islands, eroding the bank, and creating a bend.

Really twisty bends in a river are called meanders. When you're standing at a river's edge, it may be hard to see the meanders. But look at the river on a map or from the air, and you'll see all the twists and turns. Sometimes when a meander is especially curved, the river will start eroding in front of the meander and cut it off. Eventually the meander becomes a lake. Geologists call it an 'ox-bow' lake because of its U-shape.

Often a river ends its journey at the ocean. This is the mouth of the river. Here the river may dump all of the eroded rock and sand that it's been carrying. The flow of the river is blocked, and many smaller channels are formed. This area is called a delta.

Try It!

Look at a map of your area. Find the river closest to your home. Is it winding or straight? Are there any lakes nearby? Does it look as if there are any islands in the river? Can you find the river's source?

If possible, visit the river with your family. Or go to a nearby stream. What can you tell about the river or stream by the colour of the water? By the shape of the banks? By the shape of the river or stream bed? Drop a stick or leaf in the stream. Does it flow swiftly or slowly?

Part River, Part Ocean

Some rivers that run to the ocean may have wide, free-flowing mouths. These areas are called estuaries. High tides help prevent estuaries from clogging up and becoming deltas. Because an estuary is where

To see a delta for yourself, look at a map of Nigeria in northwestern Africa. Now find the River Niger. As the Niger empties into the Atlantic Ocean, the river forms a delta of more than half a dozen small channels that branch off from the big river and flow into the Gulf of Guinea. (You can also see a delta on a map of the United States that shows the Mississippi River emptying into the Gulf of Mexico.)

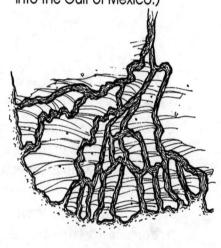

47

salt water and fresh water mix, many interesting plants, birds, fish, and other sea creatures make their home there.

An estuary also may be called a bay, a sound, or a harbour. Because they are easy for ships to reach, many estuaries have cities built near them. Unfortunately, many estuaries have been damaged by pollution and by construction of docks and channels for ships.

Still Waters

Unlike a river, a lake is a large body of water that has no direct link with an ocean. Here are some ways lakes are formed:

• Streams and rivers may be blocked by a landslide, by eroded material, by lava from a volcanic eruption, or, in some countries, by beavers, who build dams that block streams and turn forests into small lakes.

• A river meander may get cut off and form an ox-bow lake.

• A shift in the earth's crust may occur that causes a crack to appear in the earth's surface. If underground water fills up the crack, a lake may be formed.

• Many lakes in the Northern Hemisphere were formed by glaciers in the ice age. As they moved across the land, glaciers dug out low spots in the rock. Then water from the melting ice filled those low areas, creating lakes. The Great Lakes in the United States were formed by glaciers.

•Crater lakes form in the tops of ancient, extinct volcanoes. The water that fills them comes only from rain and snow.

The Life of a Lake

Most lakes exist in a state of natural balance. 'Balance' means the water that evaporates or runs off is replaced by rain, melting snow, or underground streams. The level of the lake will remain fairly consistent over time.

Lakes that rely only on rain or snowfall to replenish their water, though, may be threatened if there is an unusually dry season. In some parts of the world, a lack of rain can combine with very hot temperatures to dry up a lake completely. Even though the lake will return when the rains finally come, the absence of water for several months can threaten the lives of the animals and people who depend upon that lake for all of their water needs.

A LAKE IN DISGUISE!

The Caspian Sea in Asia isn't really a sea at all. It's a saltwater lake. And, at 1222 km long and over 1,000 metres deep, it's the world's largest lake. The world's second largest lake, Lake Superior, a freshwater lake between Michigan and Canada, isn't even close. It's only 560 km long and 400 metres deep.

Too little water can be hazardous for life in and around a lake. But too much water can be a problem as well. Sometimes lakes slowly vanish because they fill up with too much water. Heavy rains or a large snowfall leaves excess water that spills over the banks, forming streams that flow away from the lake. Over time, the streams can erode the banks of the lake to the point that most of the lake drains away.

Salty Lakes

Most lakes are supplied with fresh water from streams, underground springs, and rain or snow. But some lakes have little or no fresh water supply. In this case, lakes that used to be large are shrinking; lakes that used to be filled with fresh water have evaporated so much that the mineral and salt deposits left behind on the lake bottom have made the water as salty as the ocean.

Make Your Own Saltwater Lake!
(Whales Are Optional)

This is a summer's day project. Mix together 350 g of flour and 50 ml salt. Add water a little at a time until the dough is no longer sticky. Press the mixture into the bottom and sides of a deep, ovenproof dish.

Turn the oven on to about 100° C or Gas Mark ½. Bake the dough for 2 to 3 hours, until it becomes hard. Then carefully remove it from the oven and allow it to cool completely. This will be the lake bottom.

Slowly pour water onto the 'lake bottom' until it comes to within an inch of the top of the dough. Now set the whole thing in a quiet, sunny place on a hot day. Do a taste test of the water at noon and at 6 p.m. As the water evaporates, does it get saltier? How long does it take the lake to dry up?

Fake Lakes?

Because so many parts of the world have no freshwater rivers and lakes, people have learned how to make their own. A man-made lake is called a reservoir. A reservoir is made by building a dam on a river, which causes the river water to back up and form a lake.

Why bother with a dam? The dam controls the amount of water flowing out of the reservoir and into the river. This helps prevent flooding further downstream. Reservoir water can also be used for drinking, irrigation, and making electricity, as well as fishing, boating, and other water recreation.

Even though reservoirs are made and regulated by people, they can grow old and die just like natural lakes. Plants, fish, and sediment deposits on the reservoir bottom have to be controlled to keep the reservoir alive.

Freshwater Creatures

One-third of the fish in the world live in fresh water. Just like ocean fish, freshwater fish have adapted to different kinds of water. Trout and bullhead catfish prefer cold, fast-moving mountain streams. Perch, pike, and most other types of catfish prefer slow-running streams and lakes.

Most freshwater fish eat plants, insects, and animal remains. Only a few eat other fish or animals. The most famous flesh-eater, of course, is the piranha. Piranhas live in the rivers of South America and frequently attack livestock and humans that trespass into their waters.

Believe it or not, there are a few species of freshwater fish that can even live out of the water. Lungfish have air bladders that also work like lungs. They live in shallow water in the rain forests of Africa and South America. The mudskipper is another type of amphibious fish. It has extra-large gills and can draw oxygen from the air as well as the water. The mudskipper can also use its front fins like arms to crawl across dry land!

Man-made rivers are called canals. They are common in countries that use waterways to get people and goods from one place to another. They are also used for irrigation, to get water from a river to farms much further away.

One of the oldest canals was built by Egyptians about 4,000 years ago to join the River Nile and the Red Sea. Today, one of the most famous is the Panama Canal, which stretches across the Central American country of Panama and links the Caribbean Sea with the Pacific Ocean.

Pet Shop Fishing

Stop at a pet shop and take a look at the many varieties of fish. Most aquarium fish originally came from tropical fresh water. They are most

popular because of their large fins and bright colours.

The most common aquarium fish is the goldfish, which is a member of the carp family. But not all goldfish are gold. Some of the more unusual ones are the spotted shubunkin, the fantail, which looks like an angelfish, and the popeye, which looks just like its name!

If you're tempted to buy some fish for pets of your own, keep in mind that cherry barbs and guppies are the easiest to care for—but be warned that guppies can have as many as fifty babies a month!

The Mystery of the Lake

One of the most famous mythical creatures is said to live in Loch Ness, Scotland. Indeed, many people believe that 'Nessie' really exists.

Stories about the Loch Ness monster have been told for centuries. The earliest one was written down in the fifth century in a biography of St. Columba. Columba was a missionary to Scotland. As the story goes, Columba was standing at the edge of Loch Ness one day when he saw a monster rise up from the lake and start to attack a swimmer. Columba raised his hand and told the monster to go away. The creature obeyed.

Since then, many people have claimed to have seen the monster. Some say it looks like a snake with short legs or flippers. The few photographs that have been taken show one or more humps sticking up out of the water. But scientists haven't had much success investigating the stories because Loch Ness is a very dangerous lake. It's deep and cold, and the water is so filled with peat that divers and submarines can't see anything, even with special lights.

Most scientists say that 'Nessie' cannot exist. For one thing, no single creature could live for 1,500 years! There would have to be a monster family. But no monster bones or any other physical evidence has been found to prove that they exist.

Evidence or no evidence, people will probably continue to search for 'Nessie' for years to come.

Water in Your Own Backyard

You may not live near a river or a lake, but you probably don't have to travel very far to find a pond. A pond may be the size of a large puddle or the size of a small lake. It may be very shallow or quite deep. And ponds can be anywhere: on waste ground, in the woods, in a park. You may even have a pond in your own garden.

Ponds are formed in many of the same ways that lakes are formed. Streams and underground springs get dammed or diverted, rain and snow fill a low spot on the land. Sometimes a river floods and then goes back down again, leaving ponds and puddles. And sometimes people make their own ponds. They dig a hole and fill it with water or, if the hole is deep enough, they let the ground water fill it up.

Ponds may be smaller than oceans and lakes, but they're jammed full of living things. Pond water is usually warmer than lake water, so many more plants and small organisms have a chance to grow. In farming areas, the fertilizers farmers put on their fields wash into ponds and make even more water plants grow.

Get Wet!

If you live near a pond, you can discover pond life at close quarters for yourself. Be sure to take this book with you when you go exploring! Also take along a magnifying glass, one large jar with a lid, and three small, clear,

well-rinsed jars with lids. Mark the small jars 1, 2, and 3. Later, you will also need a microscope. (If you don't have one—and can't borrow one from a friend—ask to use one at your school's science lab.) The next few paragraphs will help you find out some fascinating things about your pond—even if you thought you knew it inside out.

The first thing to notice is the pond's colour. Does it look green or green-brown? This colour comes from algae that grow on the pond's surface. Algae are tiny plants that grow in still water. Algae would grow in swimming pools, too, if people didn't add chemicals to the water to stop it from growing. It's great for pond life, but algae's too slimy to swim in!

Once you've noticed the algae, either kneel beside the pond or wade in just up to your ankles. Now dip your large jar into the water. Scoop up some of the sediment on the bottom of the pond along with the water. Be sure also to get a sample of any material floating on top. Put the lid on the jar, and set it aside to allow the contents to settle.

While the jar is resting, look at the plants around your pond. How many different kinds of plants can you see in and around the water? Besides algae, here are some common pond plants you might see:

• Water lilies grow right on top of the water. They have a round green pad with a flower growing up from it.

• Duckweed can cover the water's surface like algae. It looks like small green leaves all bunched together. It got its name because ducks like to eat it.

• Marsh marigolds grow in the shallow water at the edge of a pond. They have bright yellow flowers.

• Reeds and rushes are long, narrow, grass-like plants that grow in the marshy edges of ponds.

• Bulrushes, also called reed mace, often grow near reeds. The long, brown and fuzzy top of each stem makes this tall marshland plant very easy to recognize.

Now kneel down at the water's edge and look closely into the pond. Can you see the bottom? Is it rocky, muddy, or sandy? If you can see the bottom, look for things that have sunk. You may see dead plants, leaves, and tree branches. You may also see the remains of fish, crayfish, and maybe some small snail shells.

Like oceans, ponds have different layers with different kinds of plants and animals in each layer. Get your three small jars. With jar 1, skim off some water from the surface. With jar 2, collect water from below the surface. (Keep the lid on the jar until you have it at the right depth.) With jar 3, collect water from the bottom of the pond. (Again, keep the lid on until the jar is at the bottom.) Put the lids on your jars. Look at each jar with the magnifying glass. What kinds of things do you see? Can you see anything swimming around? Which jar contains the most plant and animal material?

Now go back to your large jar. The heaviest material has settled on the bottom. The lightest material has floated on the top. How many layers can you see? Use your magnifying glass. Is there anything interesting hidden in the layers?

GIVE YOUR POND A GIFT!

Unfortunately, when you look at the bottom of your pond, you may also see some things that don't belong there—such as metal cans, bottles, old fishing weights, and other rubbish. Do your pond a favour by making sure you leave with everything you brought.

If your pond has already been filled with litter and rubbish, you might be able to save it. Invite some friends to help you clean out the things that don't belong in the pond and then dispose of them properly. One afternoon of caring for the pond can help turn back years of abuse. In fact, a number of forgotten and dying ponds have come back to life after caring people gave them the chance.

The Pond Food Chain

If it's summer you may have slapped away quite a few mosquitoes or midges. That's because wet places attract insects of all kinds: mosquitoes, dragonflies, water beetles, pond skaters, and spiders. Some might seem annoying, but every water insect is an important part of the pond's food chain.

Water insects lay their eggs in or near the water, and they rely on pond plants and other pond insects for their food. Likewise, fish, frogs, newts, and other pond animals rely on water insects for *their* food.

If you're very still and quiet, you may see fish pop up to the surface to feast on insects. In a pond food chain, the larger fish in the centre of the pond eat insects, while smaller minnows and tadpoles feed on plants near the water's edge. If you watch closely, you may see small schools of minnows and tadpoles huddled close to the bank.

If your pond is large enough or near a larger pond, you may see some water birds. The most common ones are ducks, coots, moorhen, and geese. They eat water plants and small fish. If you are very lucky, you may see a heron by your pond, or a kingfisher flashing past over the water. A few gulls and terns, both of which feed on fish, can be seen by large lakes.

The Tiniest Pond Creatures

After you've finished observing your pond, take your jars of pond water home for further observation. (If any of your jars have small fish or other visible water creatures in them, dump them back in the pond and collect a new sample. Most water animals are likely to die away from their habitat.)

If you have a microscope handy, you can see some tiny pond animals up close. Start with the surface water in jar 1. Use an eyedropper to collect water from the jar, and put a drop on a microscope slide. Can you see algae in the microscope? What colour and shape is it?

Examine drops from jars 2 and 3 on slides of their own. You may see some little animals wiggling and zipping around. Many of these are water fleas. They eat algae and in turn are eaten by larger insects.

Chapter 5
Water Around the World

Many Places, Many Disguises

You've already discovered that water can be fresh or salty, that it can freeze and evaporate. But water can do many more unusual things. All around the world water turns up in the most unlikely places and in the most surprising forms. But no matter what form water takes, people have always found creative ways to live with it and enjoy it.

Thar She Blows!

Every 65 minutes something happens at Yellowstone National Park, the oldest and largest national park in the United States. People say it happens so regularly that they can almost set their watches by it. It's the eruption of 'Old Faithful', one of Yellowstone's 200 geysers. A geyser is like a volcano that erupts with hot water instead of lava. Some geysers just bubble near the ground. Others shoot far into the air. 'Old Faithful' reaches up to 50 metres high. Geysers are usually found in groups. The largest groups are in Yellowstone, New Zealand, and Iceland.

TRY IT!

You can buy mineral water in the supermarket. Ask your parents to buy a bottle next time you're shopping. Look for it in the bottled water or soft-drink section. Try some. Does it taste like ordinary tap water?

Geysers are formed when river or lake water drains and flows deep underground. Because the earth gets hotter near its core, rocks far below the surface can become very hot. When the water reaches these hot rocks deep in the earth, it begins to evaporate. But the weight of the water pushing down on itself doesn't allow the water vapour room to escape. Soon the upward pressure of the vapour becomes greater than the downward pressure of the water, and BOOM! The water explodes to the surface. After the explosion, much of the water goes back down into the ground, and the whole process begins again.

A Spring's the Thing

Sometimes underground springs flow deep enough to get heated, just like geysers. But because there is more air space, an underground spring will seldom explode. Instead, heated water comes bubbling to the surface, forming pools of very warm, effervescent water. These pools, called hot springs, are popular holiday resorts, especially for older people. For centuries people have believed that the water from hot springs could cure many illnesses, like arthritis and respiratory diseases. Visitors to hot springs drink the warm water and swim in it. Two of the most famous hot springs are at Baden-Baden in Germany and Hot Springs National Park in Arkansas, USA.

Mineral springs can be hot or cold, but they always contain large amounts of minerals or gasses. The minerals wash down with rain water that seeps through the ground to the spring. Water from cold mineral springs was also believed to be good for keeping people's bodies working well.

Is It Just a Mirage?

You've seen it a hundred times: that movie scene where a man is crawling across the desert, dying of thirst, and all of a sudden he sees a pond surrounded by palm trees. Then suddenly the image shimmers and disappears. It was only a mirage.

Yet desert 'rest stops' really do exist. They're called oases. In the Sahara Desert in Africa, most oases come from underground springs. In the deserts of North America, oases are caused by rain and melting snow from nearby mountains. Some oases are big enough to provide water for whole towns. In many desert areas, people drill wells in oases and irrigate farmland with the water. As a result, desert areas that used to be dry and empty can now grow crops.

The Bedouin people, who live in the deserts of the Middle East, know how to use every part of an oasis. They travel from oasis to oasis to get water for their goats and sheep and for their families. They eat the dates that grow there and feed the date seeds to their camels. Palm leaves are used for fuel and woven into ropes and baskets. During dry seasons, many Bedouins stay near the oasis and grow crops there, using the water for irrigation.

Rivers of Ice

In the high mountains and near the North and South poles, there are frozen rivers that never thaw out. These rivers are called glaciers. Continental glaciers are very large. They cover the North pole, Antarctica, and large parts of Greenland. Valley glaciers fill up valleys in high mountains like the Alps and the Andes. They are also common in Canada and Alaska.

Glaciers are formed when the temperature is too cold for snow to melt or evaporate. Layers of snow build up and turn to ice. Even though a glacier is frozen, the ice becomes so thick and heavy that its own weight and the pull of gravity cause it to move. Most glaciers move about 30 centimetres a day. But some move much faster. As a glacier moves, it erodes the rock under it and creates a U-shaped valley.

When a glacier reaches the ocean, chunks of ice break off and fall into the water. These are called icebergs. They can be very dangerous to ships. Even though an iceberg floats, most of it lies below the surface of the water.

TRAGEDY AT SEA

In 1912, a British passenger ship called the Titanic hit an iceberg and sank on the way from England to New York City. At least 1,500 passengers drowned in the freezing water. At that time, the Titanic was the largest passenger ship ever built and everyone had believed it was also the safest. In 1985 explorers found the wreck of the Titanic off the coast of Newfoundland.

Water Is a Way of Life

All over the world there are people for whom water is more than just something to drink and wash with. These people live on the water, get food from it, play in it, travel by it, and have stories and traditions about it. Many have specially designed houses that protect them from the water around them. And all have unique and clever ways of living in their watery homes.

Houses on the Water

Imagine you woke up this morning and discovered that your house was completely surrounded by water! How would you get to school?

Your first glimpse of a lighthouse on a trip to the coast is always very exciting. Lighthouses are usually built on rocky shores. They have lamps in them that shine to warn ships away from the rocks. Today many lighthouses are lit automatically. But a hundred years ago, the lighthouse keeper and his family lived there and kept the lamp burning.

DID YOU KNOW?

Children who live in watery places usually learn to swim when they're only two or three years old. On Chinese houseboats, babies are kept on reins or have wood blocks strapped to their backs so they'll float if they fall overboard.

Where would your food come from? Where would you play? For many people around the world, home really is in the middle of the water. Some choose to live on the water because that's where their work is. Others have no choice; there isn't enough room for them to live on the land.

The city of Hong Kong is very crowded—so crowded that many people have to live in the harbour on junks, or houseboats. These houses are old fishing boats that the boat people have made into houses. Many boat people live on junks and work in the city. But many others have lived on junks their whole lives and have never set foot on land. Small merchant boats called sampans float around the harbour, selling food and clothing to the boat people.

Thailand, a country south of China, receives so much rainfall that many areas are flooded most of the time. So the Thai people build their wooden houses on stilts to raise them above the water level. The stilts are usually made from tree trunks. Each family keeps a small boat tied up to the house. In some parts of Thailand, whole villages are built on stilts. Bridges and walkways connect the houses together.

In the swampy areas of Iraq, in Asia, live people

called the Marsh Arabs. They build their houses out of the reeds that grow next to ponds and lakes. Bundles of reeds are tied together to make the walls and the curved roof. Because the ground is so muddy, the Marsh Arabs first have to cover the ground with reeds so their houses don't sink. (Recently, the Marsh Arabs have suffered special persecution, and their unique way of life is being threatened by political powers.)

Many homes are built on or near water for protection. The knights and soldiers who lived in castles in Europe centuries ago dug moats around the castles and filled them with water. The moat kept enemies from getting in through the castle door and from tunnelling under the castle. The moat was also a handy place to dump sewage. If you were an enemy soldier, would you want to swim through it to attack the castle?

A City Built on Water

The city of Venice, in north-eastern Italy, is like no other city in the world. It was built on 118 islands in the Adriatic Sea. There is so much water running through Venice, the buildings couldn't have basements or concrete foundations. Instead the whole city is built on stilts! Posts were sunk in the mud and the buildings put together on top of the posts.

Venice has few streets. The people travel from place to place along canals. There are over 150 canals in Venice. Gondolas, which look like flat-bottomed canoes, and motorboats travel along the canals like water taxicabs, taking people where they want to go. Venice holds a huge gondola race, called a regatta, every year in September.

Where the Alligators Roam

What do you think of when you hear the word *swamp*? Mud, slime, spooky moss-covered trees? Swamps can be very beautiful places. In Louisiana in the USA, they're called bayous. The French people who settled there in the 1800s named them after the French word for 'channel'. The descendants of these settlers, called Arcadians or 'cajuns', still live in the bayous. Many of them still speak French and make a living by fishing and trapping.

Another huge area of swamp in the USA is the Everglades, in Florida. Alligators, deer, turtles, pelicans, snakes, and many different kinds of fish and birds all make their home in the swamps and marshes of the Everglades.

Unlike the bayous of Louisiana, the swamps of Florida haven't had people to care for them and call them home. No people lived in the Everglades until 1842, when the Seminole Indians escaped there. The tribe was soon killed by the US Army. Then, after Florida became a state, the Everglades were nearly destroyed. The rivers flowing into the swamp were dammed to provide water for the rest of Florida. Many species of wildlife died out and many others are now endangered. In 1983 Florida began a scheme to restore the Everglades.

Home Sweet Glacier

Water takes a different form in the far north, above the Arctic Circle. Here the people have learned to live on the ice and frozen ground, called tundra. Although other groups of people live in northern Russia, Alaska, Canada, and Greenland, the Inuit people, or Eskimos, make up the majority.

Few trees and plants can grow in this cold climate, so the people get most of their food, clothing, and building materials from animals. Skins from seals, wolves, bears, and caribou are used to make warm coats, boots, and mittens. The bones of these animals are carved into tools and toys. Seal and whale blubber is used to make wax for candles and oil for lamps. The Eskimos usually dry the meat or eat it raw. When a seal or whale is killed, it's feast time.

Today most people who live in the Arctic live in towns and villages and have jobs like everyone else. But some still live as nomads, following the caribou herds and going wherever the hunting and fishing is good. Many years ago, while on their journeys, the nomads had to make houses out of whatever was available. And most of the time that meant ice and snow. Eskimos still make igloos today but they don't live in them. They use them just for overnight hunting trips.

Building an igloo takes a lot of practice. It's an art that Eskimo parents have been teaching their children for many years. They start with rectangular blocks of ice or solid snow, about 15 cm thick, set up in a circle. One end of the circle is shaved off at an angle so

BUILDING YOUR OWN IGLOO

If you get a lot of snow where you live, try building your own igloo. The Eskimo method may take a few tries to perfect, so here's an easier style of igloo.

Pile up as much snow as you can until you have a solid dome at least three or four feet high. Be sure to pack it tightly. Using a hand shovel, dig out an opening large enough to crawl through. Then start hollowing out the dome. Keep scooping out snow until your dome walls are just a few inches thick. Poke a ventilation hole in the top and drizzle some water on the outside of the igloo so it will freeze solid. You can even make a floor and a door for your igloo with plastic rubbish bags. After you and a few friends crawl inside, your igloo will soon be warm and comfortable!

the rest of the blocks can spiral up to the top. As the blocks get higher, they are tilted slightly inwards, creating a dome shape. Then a circular chunk of ice is placed on the top and a small hole cut through it for ventilation. The Eskimos dig a doorway under the igloo wall and sometimes enclose it in an ice-block tunnel. Living in an ice-house may sound cold, but it's actually quite cozy. With people and a small cooking lamp inside, the temperature can be twenty degrees higher than it is outside. But igloo dwellers don't have to worry about their homes melting: It takes a lot more heat than that to melt through 15 cm of ice!

Something to Crow About

The Arctic people naturally have lots of stories about their icy homeland. One of the most interesting is a legend about why the Arctic has six months of darkness and six months of light during the year.

Long ago, the Inuit people believe, there was only darkness. A magic crow came to visit the village and told the people that far away in the east there was daylight. The villagers begged the crow to bring them some. So the crow flew eastward and stole a ball of daylight from the people there. He brought it back to the Arctic and broke off pieces for each village. But unfortunately there wasn't enough to have daylight all year around. And so in the far north, there are six months of daylight and six months of darkness.

The Magic and Meanings of Water

Water is one of the most important parts of God's creation. Because of its role in everyday life, stories and traditions about water have sprung up all over the world.

In areas where water is scarce, people have devised some unusual rituals for getting it. Forked sticks called divining rods or dowsing rods have been used since ancient times to find underground springs. A person looking for underground streams is supposed to hold the stick by the two forks and point the long end slightly up toward the sky. As the person walks around, the stick will vibrate and bend toward the ground in the area where a well should be dug. Many people view dowsing as a superstition, but science has yet to explain why some of those who dowse for water actually find it.

On the other hand, science *has* explained what makes rain. But that hasn't kept people from carrying on the rainmaking traditions of their ancestors. Some groups, such as the American Indians, stress the importance of ancient rituals and continue to hold 'rain dances', ceremonies to ask earth spirits to bring rain for their crops.

Seas and rivers hold special religious meanings for many cultures. The ancient Scandinavians put their people who had died in small boats and set them adrift on the sea. They believed the boats would carry the dead people to Valhalla, or heaven. In Japan, people still light paper lanterns to honour the souls of those who have died. They float the lanterns on a river, which carries the lights to the sea. The travelling lanterns symbolize the journey of souls from this world to the world beyond death.

Washing with water also has a special meaning. In the Bible, God commanded the Hebrew people to wash themselves before they came into the temple to worship him. That's not because God didn't want filthy people in his temple! Washing did remove the dust of the desert, of course, but it also reminded the Hebrews that God is pure and holy. By washing before they came into God's presence, they reminded themselves that God is perfect, without any stain of evil or wrongdoing.

Later Jesus Christ, God's Son, used washing with water to symbolize the washing away of people's sins. This tradition is called baptism. Christians today are still baptized as a sign of their commitment to God.

Try It!

Does your family take holidays by the sea, or on rivers or canals? Have you been skiing? Or skating? Do you enjoy rowing? Or swimming? Competitive water sports? Synchronised swimming? Make a scrapbook for your family with information on these water 'experiences'. Add photos, and write comments and quotes as a record for the family to keep and enjoy.

Chapter 6
Water at Work

From fishing to washing, from manufacturing to travelling—since the world began, people have put water to work for them. In the earliest days, rivers and oceans gave people food. Rain and groundwater irrigated their crops. Lakes, rivers, and seas became 'highways' to carry people and goods from one place to another. And although industries began to change the way people did these simple tasks early in the 1900s, even the most complicated machinery can't replace water altogether when it comes to doing hard work.

Food for All

Nearly every culture in the history of the world has developed its own ways of catching fish. Even though you might not like it, the people in some countries eat fish at nearly every meal. But not everyone lives near a good fishing ground. So, to meet the demand for fish around the world, many countries export their fish to places where they are not as plentiful.

How is all this fishing done? People who live near oceans and lakes use a variety of nets and traps. Some nets, such as seine nets and skimming nets, are used near the shore. The fisherman wades in, casts out the net, and pulls it in by hand. Other nets are pulled by boats. Trawling is the most popular method of fishing. A boat drags a large net, called a trawl, across the ocean floor, trapping fish as the net sweeps through the water.

Other sea creatures must be caught with baited traps. Lobster pots and crab traps have funnel-shaped openings, so the creatures can get in but not out. Some tribal people in Africa and South America catch fish in baskets. They also build rock walls in shallow water to catch fish that get washed in by tides.

River fishing calls for a different approach. One of the earliest methods of fishing was with spears. Do you think you could throw a spear fast enough to nab a fish before it swims away? For centuries the fishing rod has been the most popular method of fishing in rivers. The real 'anglers' know just the right place for a good catch, and exactly the right bait, or fishing fly to use. This is a peaceful pastime, a popular sport and can be very competitive.

Fish Farming

Some parts of the ocean and rivers have been fished so much—for so long—that there aren't many fish left. To solve this problem, in many countries fish hatcheries breed different kinds of fish from eggs and then release them into nearby rivers and lakes. This keeps the rivers and lakes from getting overfished. (Phone your local council or river authority to find out if there is a fish hatchery near your town.)

In other areas, pollution has killed off the fish. Fish farming has become a popular way of coping with that situation. But fish farming—using enclosed tanks and special diets to grow fish for food—is nothing new: the idea began in China many centuries ago. Now many countries are raising fish in farms as well as using boats and nets in open water.

The frozen shrimps you buy at the supermarket may have come from a shrimp farm. There are many shrimp farms in the United States near the Gulf of Mexico and in South America. Farmers in China and other Asian countries often combine shrimp farming and rice farming. Flooded rice paddy fields are good places for shrimps to grow too.

Water for the Fields

In most countries of the world, farmers cannot rely on getting just the right amount of rain at just the right time for their crops. They must somehow get water from the nearest river or lake to their fields, a process called irrigation. Today, industrialized countries use pumps and sprinkler systems to irrigate their crops. For instance, you are irrigating on a small scale when you water your lawn and garden. But many much older techniques are also still used around the world.

For centuries, farmers along the River Nile in Africa have used a *shaduf* to get water from the river. A shaduf is a long pole with a bucket on the end of it that is suspended over the water. The farmer lowers the pole and bucket into the river, pulls water out, turns the pole, and dumps the water either into buckets or irrigation canals on the other side. Because this system relies solely on human muscle, it can take a very long time to water an acre of land.

Two more recent developments in irrigation are canals and dams. Farmers may dig canals, or ditches, from a river or lake directly to their fields. A special gate controls the amount of water that flows into the fields. Damming a river holds back water that can be piped or channelled to farms for irrigation. A dam also keeps rivers from flooding or drying up in a drought; it controls the amount of water that flows into the river.

Too Much, Too Little

Humans have invented many methods of controlling where water goes and where it doesn't go. But no matter how hard we try to manage water, it doesn't always cooperate.

Too much water can be disastrous. Floods can happen when heavy rains or too much melting snow cause rivers to overflow. Hurricanes and tidal waves on the ocean can also flood coastal areas. And when a poorly built dam breaks, the huge mass of water that gushes out will wipe out anything in its path.

Some of the worst floods in living memeory happened at Lynmouth and Lynton in Devon in 1952, when the swollen River Lyn completely destroyed large parts of the villages as it swept down carrying huge rocks and boulders and uprooted trees. In January the following year, the East Coast of England also suffered massive floods as the sea broke through sea-defences.

Too little water can be destructive too. A drought occurs when too little rain falls. Ponds and streams dry up, and crops die because they cannot be irrigated. Eventually people die too. Eastern Africa has been suffering from a drought for years. Millions of people have died because of it.

Sometimes people are as much to blame for floods and droughts as the weather. At certain times every year parts of Bangladesh are destroyed by floods. Hundreds of people die and much of the land is ruined. At other times Bangladesh receives very little water. Crops die and the people don't have enough food. The problem is the Ganges River. It starts in India and flows through Bangladesh to the ocean. But India and Bangladesh cannot agree on who owns the Ganges River. Each country won't let the other build the necessary dams to control the flow of the river. And so, every year, people along the Ganges suffer.

In some parts of the world where flooding occurs frequently, people have found ways to protect themselves and their homes. Levees are banks of earth built up along rivers to keep out floodwater. These embankments are sometimes built out of concrete. Dams and reservoirs can control the flow of excess water, while digging out river channels makes them bigger so they can hold more water. And scientists have found that

MAKE YOUR OWN WATER-POWERED BOAT

To start, you'll need some large chunks of thick polystyrene and an empty cardboard milk carton. Cut two pieces of polystyrene 2 cm by 20 cm. Cut another piece 7.5 cm square. (It cuts easiest if you make a shallow cut with a sharp knife and then snap the sections apart with your hands.)

Lay the long pieces on either side of the square, with the top ends even with the top of the square. Attach them with rubber bands. Then cut two 2 x 7.5 cm pieces from the milk carton. Hold one of the pieces horizontally and make a 1 cm slit at the midpoint. Do the same with the other piece. Now insert the two pieces together at the slits. This is the water wheel.

Loop one rubber band over the centre of the wheel and position the wheel between the two long pieces. Pull one end of the rubber band over one piece and the other end over the remaining piece.

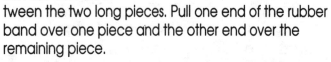

To make the boat go, wind the wheel backwards so the rubber band twists. Hold the wheel tightly until you put in the water. Then let it go!

Use toothpicks to attach paper people, flags, or an upper level to your paddle-wheel boat.

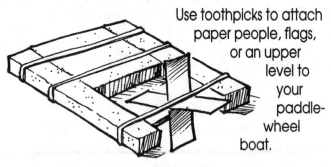

replanting forests along riverbanks keeps floodwater from spreading and eroding the soil.

Water Power

What do a toy boat and a generator of electric power have in common? They both depend on the flow of water for their 'power'. Harnessing the power of moving water is another way people make water work for them. One of the first machines that was able to put water power to use was the water wheel.

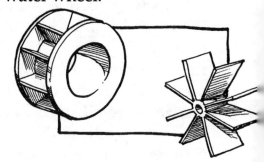

There are two different kinds of water wheels. An undershot wheel has paddles that stick out and are pushed by the water. The boat described on the left uses an undershot wheel. On a real boat, the flow of the river pushes the paddles and the wheel moves the boat.

An overshot wheel has paddles that are shaped like buckets. Water must pour from a stream or trough onto the top of the wheel. The water fills the top buckets and pushes them down. This type of wheel is most commonly used in mills. Country areas are good places to look for old mills with overshot water wheels. In the 18th and 19th centuries, flour mills used water wheels to turn the grindstone that ground grain into flour.

In the 20th century, people used the idea of the water wheel to make more complicated machinery. The turbine is a water wheel made of metal. Turbines can be turned by water, gas, or steam. Water-powered turbines are used in hydroelectric power plants.

How do you get power from a moving wheel? Turbines are attached to generators. As the flowing water turns the turbine, the generators are activated, producing electricity. Because of their need for moving water, hydroelectric power plants are usually located near waterfalls or dams.

Moving Along

Long before the invention of aeroplanes, people discovered that it often took less time and trouble to transport things by water than by land.

But transporting by waterway isn't always easy. Sometimes rocks, waterfalls, rapids, and even chunks of land can get in the way. So people built canals that could carry the boats and barges around the problem areas. Two of the most famous canals are the Panama Canal in Central America and the Suez Canal in northern Africa.

The Panama Canal connects the Atlantic Ocean and the Caribbean Sea. It's 82 kilometres long and transports more than 10,000 ships a year—more than any other canal. Many of the ships travel from the east coast of the United States to California. Going all the way down to Panama may seem out of the way, but without the Panama Canal, the ships would have to sail all the way around the southern tip of South America!

The Suez Canal is 160 kilometres long and connects the Mediterranean Sea and the Red Sea. European countries use it to transport goods to and from Asia.

Because some bodies of water are higher or lower than others, canals sometimes have to go uphill or downhill. Many canals have a system of locks, similar to steps, that help the ships make a smooth journey from one level of water to another. Locks are a series of enclosed chambers in which the water level can be raised or lowered. After a ship enters the first chamber, the water level goes up or down to match the level in the second chamber. The ship moves on until it reaches the water level at the end of the canal.

The Essential Ingredient

Take a look at the objects around you. Just about everything you see was made with at least a little bit of water. Most industries couldn't get by without water. Some use it just to wash their equipment and buildings. For other industries, water is the main ingredient in their product.

The paper that this book was printed on is 7% water! It was made from wood pulp and some recycled paper. It takes at least 100 times as much water as pulp to make paper. A big Sunday newspaper, for example, takes about 350 litres of water to make. The wood pulp and recycled paper are dumped into huge vats of water to soak. Then the pulp travels on a conveyor belt while the water is squeezed out of it. Rollers flatten it. Then it dries and is rolled on huge spools.

Water also is used by companies that mould products from metal. First, it is used to separate the different parts of the metal after it is mined. Later, water is used to cool off metal that has been melted and shaped into something useful. It takes 240,000 litres of water to make one tonne of steel.

In Your Own Kitchen Sink

Where does the water in your house come from? For most people, it comes from your local water company.

The water is taken from rivers and boreholes and, after being cleaned, is pumped into a large storage tank or underground reservoir. From the storage tank, main supply pipes, called water mains, carry the water to each street. Smaller pipes, buried about one metre underground, go from the water main to each building. Most storage reservoirs are built either on hills or on top of towers, so that gravity will increase the water pressure and help the water to flow throughout the pipe system.

Water flowing downwards has enough pressure to travel up from underground into your house. But water can't travel uphill very far without help. So if you live in an area with lots of steep hills, or in a block of flats, your water probably gets pumped to you. Pumps are also needed where the water pressure has to be greater than normal. Without a pump, a fire hose spraying water from a hydrant could only spray a few yards. Imagine how hard a pump has to work to spray water several storeys high! A few houses in remote areas get their water from a well or a nearby

HOW MUCH WATER?

Water is used to produce many products that people use every day. Consider how much water it takes to make these familiar things:

1 litre of milk — *80 litres of water*

1 package of rice — *640 litres of water*

1 can of fruit — *9 litres of water*

1 litre of petrol — *20 litres of water*

4 rubber car tyres — *nearly 500,000 litres of water*

HOMEMADE WATER TOWER

You'll need two 2-pint paper milk cartons and two plastic bendy straws. Punch a small hole near the top of each milk carton. Insert the longer end of each straw into each hole. Bend the straws and connect them by pinching the end of one and putting it inside the other. Now fill the first milk carton with water. What happens to the water when the carton is filled?

HARD OR SOFT?

Is your water hard or soft? Hold your hands under a running tap. Then rub them together. Do they feel sticky? Then your water is hard. Do they feel slippery? Then your water is soft. You can also test by squirting some shampoo or liquid soap on your wet hands. Does the soap lather a lot? Does it seem hard to rinse off completely? Then your water is soft. Soap doesn't lather well in hard water.

spring in the hills. This water has to be checked by the water authority to see whether it contains any impurities or bugs.

If you have well water, a pipe runs from your house down to the aquifer, or water table, which is the level where ground water collects, deep down under the earth. The well pump pulls the water up and pumps it through the various pipes in your house.

What's In Your Water?

Underground water is generally clean and safe to drink because the soil filters out impurities. But sometimes it contains iron and other minerals and metals. Water with lots of minerals and metals in it is called 'hard water.' Water that has had these minerals and metals removed is called 'soft water.'

When you wash up in hard water, the minerals mix with the soap and leave a dirty scum. The same can happen when washing your skin and hair with hard water. (For this reasons, some people have water softeners installed in their plumbing systems.) Rain water is the softest water of all, because it hasn't travelled through the ground and picked up any minerals along the way.

Occasionally water becomes contaminated by chemicals that are dumped on the ground and into nearby streams. Well water needs to be tested once a year and treated if it's contaminated. Piped water goes through a water treatment plant to remove impurities before it reaches its destination. A chemical called chlorine, which is found in bleach, is added to kill bacteria. Swimming pool water has lots of chlorine added to it—to keep the water clean even during heavy use.

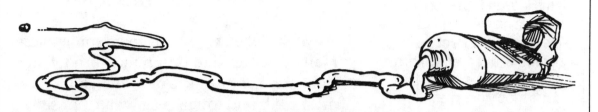

THE TOOTH ABOUT FLUORIDE

Another chemical added to the water supply is fluoride—the same stuff that's in toothpaste. In the 1930s scientists discovered that people who had natural fluoride in their water had fewer cavities. So water companies have gradually introduced fluoride to their water supply, even though some people didn't want extra things in their water. Fluoridation is still controversial. It's expensive, and some dentists and doctors feel it isn't necessary anymore because most toothpastes have fluoride. Doctors have even discovered that too much fluoride can discolour teeth and cause bone disease.

How Much Are You Washing Away?

Guess which one thing in your house uses the most water. The washing machine? The shower? Nowhere near. It's the toilet. Each flush uses 22 litres of water. If your family flushes 10 times a day, that's more than 200 litres. The average bath only requires about 110 litres. (Short showers use less.) One load of laundry takes 136 litres. Washing your hands uses 2 litres. And water runs from a tap at about 12 litres per minute.

TRY IT!

Keep a 'water use' log for one week. Have each person in your family record the water they use: every time they flush the toilet, have a bath, use the washing machine, wash their hands, get a drink, take a shower, and so on. Use the statistics above to get an approximate amount of water used. At the end of the week look at your results. Are you surprised at how much water you use?

Old Water into New

All this used water has to go somewhere. Many cities used to pump their used water right into nearby lakes or rivers. But today in most cities and towns, used water, or sewage, travels to a sewage treatment plant. There it sits in tanks until the larger, heavier materials in the water, called sludge, have settled to the bottom. After the sludge is removed, the water is sprayed over gravel beds to remove smaller impurities. Bacteria are added to the water to eat up the dissolved materials. After this, the water is tested for purity and, if it passes, gets put back into a river, lake, or reservoir.

Some rural households aren't on mains drainage and so collect waste in a cesspool, regularly emptied, or have a septic tank which is like a small sewage treatment plant. Used water goes into an underground tank while the sludge settles. Bacteria help break down the sludge and the water drains off onto gravel which filters the water before it seeps into the soil and down into the ground.

TRY IT!

Making your own water filter will help you see how sand and rocks can actually clean water. You'll need a disposable plastic dish (a large margarine tub is good), a glass bowl, a handful of gravel, 2 paper coffee filters, a cup of sand, and at least two cups of filthy, muddy water. Punch a few holes in the bottom of the tub, and lay the coffee filters in the bottom of the dish. Next add the sand, then the gravel. Set the dish into the glass bowl. Then slowly pour the dirty water over the top of the gravel. Watch it as it seeps out. Is it cleaner than it was? (Though the water may look clean, this filter system does not kill the germs in the water—so don't try to drink it!)

A Wet Job, but Somebody's Got to Do It!

Water accomplishes a lot of tasks, but it takes people to put water to work for the world. The following list of occupations involve working with water in some way.

meteorologist	diver	fisher
weather forecaster	lifeguard	dock worker
marine biologist	skier, ski resort worker	ship builder
aquarium worker	sea explorer	car-wash attendant
fish hatchery worker	ice skater, hockey player	window cleaner
chemist	sailor	washer-up
water scientist	surfer	plumber
botanist	water skier	farmer
gardener	firefighter	water-treatment plant
doctor	naval officer	worker
nutritionist	Coast Guard	paper-mill worker
geologist	ocean liner crewmember	recycling-plant worker
environmentalist	boat, ship,	hydroelectric engineer
swimmer	or submarine crew	chef

One famous person loved his water occupation so much that he changed his name in honour of it.

Samuel Langhorn Clemens, better known as Mark Twain, was a journalist who started out as a riverboat captain on the Mississippi River. When he began writing humorous columns for the newspaper, he wanted to use a memorable name. He chose 'Mark Twain,' which is riverboat talk meaning 'the water is two fathoms deep here.'

Chapter 7
Water at Play

Water moves things, water feeds things, and water washes things. But water is also fun! We can splash it, float on it, jump into it, and chuck it at each other. When it freezes, we can build things out of it, throw it, roll around in it, and slide on it. No matter what the season, there is always something fun to do with water. What's your favourite water, snow, or ice activity? Read on—you'll probably find out something new about it!

Take the Plunge

Who invented swimming? Probably the first person who ever watched a fish and wished she could flip around in the water too. Swimming is something anyone can learn. You don't have to be athletic or have special equipment. But you do have to follow a few safety rules:

1. Never go swimming alone. Make sure an adult who swims well is with you. If you're at a public pool, a lifeguard should be on duty.

2. Don't go swimming if you are tired or have just eaten a big meal. You certainly can't swim well if you're drowsy.

3. Don't jump into cold water. Go in gradually so your body can get used to the temperature change.

4. Only a trained lifeguard should try to rescue a swimmer who is in trouble. Don't jump in yourself unless you have been trained in lifesaving. If you see someone who needs help, call a lifeguard. If a life belt or something else that floats is available, throw it out to the swimmer.

Survival Swimming

Whether you're a beginner or an expert, it's good to remember that even the best swimmers can have trouble in an emergency. But the key to handling emergencies in the water is to be prepared.

Think back to Chapter 3, where you read about fish with air bladders. You can float with 'air bladders' too—your lungs.

Try this in shallow water first. Stand up in the water, take a deep breath, and hold it. Then relax your body, lean your head forward, and let your feet rise off the bottom. The air in your lungs will make you float to the surface. Let the air out through your nose, then quickly lift your chin above the water and take another breath. If you practise this technique every time you go swimming, you'll be ready in an emergency.

Swimming for Sport

It wasn't until the 1800s that swimming actually became a sport. Now swimming competitions are held all over the world for swimmers of all ages and levels. The most prestigious, of course, is the Olympics. There are many swimming events in the Olympics. They vary in the length of the races and the types of strokes used. Some events are relays, involving more than one swimmer. Swimmers from many countries train for

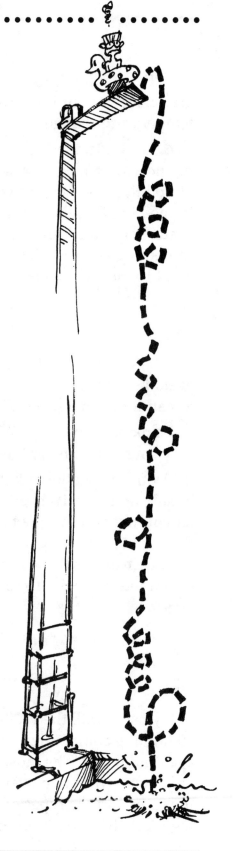

four years just to participate in a few Olympic races.

Getting into the water is as much a sport today as swimming through it. People in island countries have been diving from cliffs for centuries. (Of course, these divers have to know what's under the water they're diving into!) Today, in competitive diving, divers jump from either a springboard or a platform. A springboard is the kind of bouncy diving board you see at most pools. A platform is stationary and stands 10 metres above the water. Divers do several different kinds of dives and are judged by how precise their movements are and how smoothly they go into the water.

Underwater Sightseeing

Setting records and winning medals aren't the only benefits of swimming. As you know by now, there are plenty of fascinating things to see underwater in lakes and oceans. Snorkelling is a fun and, with a little practice, an easy way to get a glimpse of the underwater world. You need only flippers, a mask, and a snorkel. A snorkel is a J-shaped breathing

TRY IT!

With a little imagination, basketball, soccer, badminton, volleyball and many other sports and games can be adapted for the water. Get together with your friends and invent your own water game. (How about water table tennis?)

tube. One end fits in your mouth, and the other end sticks up out of the water.

Snorkelling takes practice. Contact your local sports centre and see if they offer classes. (Be warned: you'll probably get a few mouthfuls of water through the snorkel at first.) When you've mastered the technique you may be able to go snorkelling while on holiday—preferably abroad, if you want to stay in the water any length of time.

Scuba diving is a lot like snorkelling except you can swim deeper and take extra air along with you. 'Scuba' stands for 'Self-Contained Under-water Breathing Apparatus'. The extra air is contained in oxygen tanks that are strapped to your back. With the help of the oxygen, and special rubberized suits called wetsuits, scuba divers can explore deep lakes and oceans. Scuba diving can be a fun sport for the whole family, but you may have to wait a few years before you can try it: if you're interested, find out more from your local club.

Water Games

Just about any form of tag that can be played on land can be played in water, too. And sometimes it's a lot more fun! One of the most popular water games is 'Marco Polo', which is just like blindman's bluff. The 'blindman' closes his or her eyes and walks through the water calling 'Marco!' while the other players answer 'Polo!' The 'blindman' follows the sounds of the voices and tries to touch another player. Walking through water is awkward—so getting away from the 'blindman' can be a challenge! (One variation allows the 'Polo' players to dive underwater and swim to a new location. Of course, you and your friends can play by whatever rules you want—as long as you all agree what they are!)

Many sports can also be played in the water. One of the most popular official water sports is water polo. It's similar to soccer or hockey, but it is played in a swimming pool. The object is to try to score by throwing or pushing a rubber ball into the goal net. Each team has a goalie and six field players. You can either pass the ball or swim with it. A game consists of five 20-minute periods. Try water polo in the shallow end of the pool. The real pros play in deep water. How long do you think you could jump around in deep water before getting tired?

Catch a Wave

Swimming and diving are great, but there are lots of ways to have fun on top of the water, too. Two sports that have been around for decades are water skiing and surfing. If you've ever tried either sport, you know they're hard—but a lot of fun once you get the hang of them.

Water skiing is a lot like snow skiing. Many of the same moves are used, but water skiers of course must depend on a speedboat to pull them. Professional water skiers can ski over jumps, hold the tow bar with one foot, and even make human pyramids on skis!

Surfers rely on the power of waves rather than the power of a boat. Because of that, you can't do much regular surfing if you don't live near the sea, or a surfing beach. What's needed are large waves and sandy beaches. Cornwall and Pembrokeshire have the best beaches. The basic techniques of surfing aren't hard to learn—but they take some skill to master! The surfer must learn how to paddle into a wave while lying down on a surfboard, stand up on the board, and ride the wave until it crests and breaks on the beach. Or until he or she falls off!

In the 1960s, two surfers who also enjoyed sailing decided to combine the two sports by putting a sail on a surfboard. The result was windsurfing, a sport now enjoyed by people all over the world.

Sailing, Sailing

In many countries, boating is not just a way to travel or catch fish. It's become a sport. There are probably as many different kinds of boats as there are different kinds of water.

Canoeing is one of the most popular kinds of boating. People canoe on rivers or in lakes. Because no motor or sail is pushing you along, you can take your time in a canoe and enjoy the sights. And because a canoe is a quiet boat, you may see unusual birds, and other wildlife in the area that would usually be frightened by the sounds of a boat.

If you've ever read books about sailing ships, explorers, and pirates, you know that sailors have a language all their own. Here are some terms you've probably heard but may not have understood.

Bow - the front of the boat

Stern - the back of the boat

Forward - towards the bow

Aft - towards the stern

mast - the pole that holds up the sails

mainsail - the largest sail

jib - a small sail at the front of the boat

boom - on a small sailing boat, the horizontal pole attached to the mast

sheet - any rope on the boat

halyard - a rope used for raising and lowering a sail

setting the sails - to move the sails so they catch the wind

keeling - when the boat tips sideways

knot - a measure of distance and speed on the water. One knot means one nautical mile (1,852 m) per hour.

Rafting is usually done on rivers. For rafters, the rougher the river, the more fun it is! White-water rafting is done in rivers with a lot of rapids.

Kayaking is another sport for fast-running rivers. A kayak is an enclosed canoe with a hole just large enough for one person to sit in. The kayak was invented centuries ago by native people in the arctic. Kayaking takes a lot of practice. You have to learn how to paddle, how to steer, and how to turn upright when you and your kayak roll upside down in the water. Kayaking is such a challenging sport, it was made an official Olympic event.

Larger boats need larger bodies of water. Sailing is a sport popular on lakes, reservoirs, and on the sea. Sailing takes some practice. The sail must be moved quickly in different directions to catch the wind in just the right way. But sailing is just as much fun to watch, too, because the boats are so beautiful and graceful.

Let's Get Wet!

What's more fun than getting sprayed with water on a hot day? Spraying somebody else, of course! There are lots of ways to have fun with water at home. So if it's hot and you don't live near a swimming pool, put on your swimsuit and get out the garden hose!

CARE FOR THE LAND

In some parts of Great Britain there has been severe drought over the past few years. Not enough rain has fallen, and too much water has been taken out of rivers as demand has gone up.

Do not use your garden hose if there is a ban in your area. Check it out.

Make Your Own Splashing Sprinkler

Your family may have some sort of sprinkler attachment that they use to water the lawn and garden. If they don't, you can make your own. Use a small nail to carefully poke holes in a one-litre plastic bottle. The bottle will be laid on its side on the ground, so you only need holes on one side of it. Ask an adult to help you make several slits with a sharp knife in the top of the bottle. Squeeze the top together and fit it into the end of a garden hose. Wrap some parcel tape around the connection. Then turn on the hose and get ready to get wet!

Even if you don't have access to a hose and sprinkler, you can still get wet—and get your friends wet too. For instance, there are dozens of different kinds of squirt guns on the market—from cheap water pistols to expensive high-tech water blasters. But no matter what they cost or how fancy they look, all squirt guns and spray bottles work the same way.

TRY IT!

Get a tall glass of water and two plastic straws. Put one straw in the glass. It should be no more than 1 cm higher than the glass, so cut it off if it's too long. Hold the straw in the glass with one hand. Hold the second straw over the first at a right angle so the ends meet. Now blow in the second straw. What happens to the water in the first straw? Now blow really hard. The water in the first straw should spray out.

A squirt gun and spray bottle work on the same principle. A tube extends from the nozzle into the container of water. Normally the air pushing down inside the tube is the same as the air pushing down on the liquid in the bottle. But when you pump or pull the trigger, air is pushed over the top of the tube. This air isn't as strong as the air pushing down on the liquid. In other words, the air pressure in the tube is reduced. So the liquid rises in the tube and squirts out of the nozzle.

Hit the Slopes

In countries where there is winter snow, people worked out a long time ago that it's quicker and easier to slide over the snow than to trudge through it. Skiing, like boating, is another form of transport that has become a sport. There are two types of skiing: alpine (downhill) and nordic (cross-country).

Alpine skiers wear sturdy, supportive boots to protect their ankles. The boots clamp onto the skis at the toe and heel. By pointing the skis different ways and using the inside and outside edges, downhill skiers can go straight, turn, and zig-zag down mountain slopes.

Nordic skiing is a lot like walking. For this reason, cross-country ski boots aren't clamped down at the heel like downhill boots. The boots, which are more like shoes, attach to the ski at the toe. The skis are lighter and narrower than downhill skis. They are specially treated so that the skis glide forward but not backward.

What do you think is the skier's most important piece of equipment? Believe it or not, it's wax. Downhill skiers rub or melt wax onto the bottom of their skis to make them more slippery. But cross-country skiers wax their skis to make them grip the snow better. Skis behave different ways in different types of snow. So different types of wax must be used to adapt to various snow conditions.

TRY IT!

Snow skiing is a lot more like waterskiing than you might think. Get an ice cube and a piece of string. Lay the string across the top of the ice cube and pull down on the ends. Keep pulling for a few minutes. The pressure of the string is melting the ice. If the ice cube stays cold, it will refreeze and the string will look as if it's been threaded through the ice cube.

For the same reason, skis don't actually slide on snow. When they push down, they create friction which rapidly melts a thin layer of surface snow. For a fraction of a second, the skis are really sliding on water!

Skiing didn't become a sport until about 1850. At that time the first ski races were held in Norway and in the Alps. Today the major competitions are the winter Olympics, the World Championships, and the World Cup. Downhill racing and slalom skiing are the main events in the alpine competitions. In the slalom, skiers must zig-zag around flexible poles.

Ski jumping and freestyle jumping are two of the most fascinating events to watch. Jumpers use special cross-country skis and no poles. They are judged mostly on distance. Freestyle jumping began in the 1960s, and is also called 'hotdog' skiing. Freestyle skiers jump off of short ramps and do somersaults and twists in the air be-

Archaeologists in Sweden have found a preserved ski and some rock carvings of skiers that are at least 5,000 years old. And in Scandinavian mythology, the Vikings even had a god and goddess of skiing!

RIDING FROZEN WAVES

The latest craze to hit the slopes is snowboarding, a combination of surfing and skateboarding on the snow. Snowboarders ski on one wide ski. Special tracks that look like frozen waves are dug in the snow, and snowboarders ski the walls like a skateboard ramp.

fore landing on their skis. Freestyle jumping has just become an official Olympic sport. Many professional skiers think it's 'show-off' skiing, but freestylers continue to try to get recognition for their sport.

In a One-Horse Open Sleigh

Sleighs, sleds and toboggans have been around for centuries. The earliest ones were used in northern Europe and arctic areas to carry game and hunting supplies across the snow. But sleds were even used in areas with little snow, pulled across the grass and sand.

Homemade sleds have been common since the 1700s, but the first commercial sleds were produced in 1870. They had rigid wooden or iron runners and no steering bar. A few years later, moveable runners and steering bars were added. Eventually sled manufacturers curved the backs of the runners for safety.

Sledding as a racing sport was invented in the 1800s by British people who were on holiday in the Alps. Since then the sled has been redesigned and fine-tuned to achieve maximum speed. In the Olympics, the two main sledding events are the luge and the bobsled.

A luge is a one-person toboggan with metal runners. The riders lie on their backs and lean back and forth to steer down the long, winding track. Luge riders point their toes and wear special suits to cut down on wind resistance. They can travel as fast as 130 km per hour! A bobsled is an enclosed sled with two sets of runners. Bobsleds have seats for either two or four riders. The rider in front steers, the rider in back handles the emergency brake, and the other riders help steer by leaning their bodies.

For the average kid who wants to hit the sled

hill, the options for sleds are almost unlimited. The old wooden sleds with metal runners are still around. Their advantage is that you can steer them. But they can be dangerous if you collide with a tree or another person. Wooden toboggans can be steered only by shifting your weight; you need a powdery, even slope with few bumps for a good toboggan ride. Inner tubes, especially the big kind from tractors and aeroplanes, can really fly, and you can fit more than one person in the centre hole if the tube is big enough. But if you hit a bump, you'll be airborne!

MUSH! MUSH!

Native people in arctic lands use dogs instead of horses to pull their sleds. The Iditarod is a 1,690-km dogsled race from Anchorage to Nome, Alaska. It takes place in late winter. The Iditarod is run on a trail that used to be used to carry mail and supplies to small Alaskan towns. Forest rangers in Alaskan parks still use dogsleds to patrol the parks in the winter.

The most popular and inexpensive sleds today are plastic toboggans. They are also the safest, because they are small enough to control by leaning and dragging your feet, and they don't bounce too high if you hit a bump. Many plastic toboggans today are built like mini-bobsleds, with a brake handle and a steering wheel that turns small plastic runners.

TRY IT!

What's your favorite kind of sled? Do you prefer the kind with runners, a plastic or wooden toboggan, or an old inner tube? If you live where it snows, experiment to find the fastest sled. Think about what you've learned about snow. How much pressure is needed to melt the surface snow? Do some kinds of sleds create too much friction and slow you down? How can you cut down on wind resistance with your clothes and body position? Have a contest with your friends to see who can come up with the most creative sled. How about a plastic tray? A cardboard box? Or an old towel rubbed stiff with wax?

Sliding on the Ice

Just as a ski melts surface snow, an ice skate melts the ice and glides along on water. Long ago people skated on frozen rivers and canals to get from one place to another. Today people have made ice skating a sport and an art.

Figure skating is a lot more than just dancing on the ice. The sport got its name because figure skaters were required to cut 'figures' into the ice with the blades of their skates. Figure skate blades are flat with sharp edges. They have notches cut into the toe of the blade to help the skaters stop and turn quickly. Figure skating is one of the most popular events at the winter Olympics. Athletes skate alone or in pairs. In the 1976 Olympics, ice dancing was added as an event. Ice dancing has fewer required figures and more dance moves.

Speed skaters wear skates with extra-long blades that help them travel faster—sometimes as fast as 48 km per hour. In the Olympics, speed skaters race against each other but are also timed. The skater with the lowest time wins the medal. Speed skating races take place on an oval track, and there are different races for different lengths.

Ice hockey is like slippery soccer. Instead of a ball, the six players on each team hit a rubber disc, or 'puck', with a curved stick. Hockey skates are similar to speed skates except the blades are shorter. Hockey players must wear lots of padding. When you're chasing a puck across the ice, it's hard not to crash into somebody or something!

Fun for a Winter Day

You can have fun in the snow or on the ice with skis, sleds, skates, or no equipment at all. But whatever you're doing in the winter weather, you'll have more fun if you follow a few safety tips:

1. Don't throw snowballs at cars or at people's heads. Aim for padded areas instead—like your friend's back!

2. Wrap up warm. Don't stay out if your fingers and toes start getting cold and numb. Once inside, warm up gradually if you want to avoid chilblains.

3. Don't step on to a frozen pond or lake unless you're sure it's frozen solid. Be sure to take an adult with you.

4. If you want to keep warm—and help Mum and Dad at the same time—offer to clear the pathways and the pavement in front of your house or an elderly neighbour's house.

TRY IT!

What can you do with the snow in your garden? Here are some suggestions for winter fun with your friends.

● Fill the yard with snow angels. If you've never made one, just lie on your back in the snow and move your arms and legs up and down. Then try to stand up without messing up your pattern. For a change of pace, try making a snow angel lying face down!

● Play snow tag. Walk out a big circle in the snow. Make three lines going across it like spokes on a wheel. All players must stay on the lines while the person who is 'It' tries to catch them. The centre is 'safe'.

● Paint a ball with bright, fluorescent paint. Have a game of soccer in the snow.

● Don't just settle for plain old snow forts and snowpeople. Reach for new heights in creativity! Make a snow hippo instead—or a duck or a robot or anything you can think of. Because snow holds a shape better when it's wet, sprinkle extra water on your sculpture if your snow is too dry to pack. You can add colour to your sculpture by painting on food colouring mixed with water. Have a snow sculpture contest in your road.

Chapter 8
Water Pollution and Conservation

Did you know that there is the same amount of water on the earth today as there was when the earth was created? Water can't disappear. It continually evaporates, rises, and comes back down again. So why is everyone so concerned about water conservation these days? The amount of water on earth has stayed the same, but the number of people hasn't. Because the earth's population is always growing, there is less water for each person to use and more of it being polluted.

Too Much Here, Too Little There

The amount of water in an area depends on how much rain and snow it gets. In some parts of the world, like deserts, water is naturally scarce. Other parts of the world, like tropical rainforests, have more than enough water. Uneven water distribution is just a fact of life on earth.

When a water crisis happens, many people think the world is running out of water. But this will never happen. In the past ten years some parts of Great Britain have had water shortages. There has been not enough rainfall and too much water has been taken out of rivers by industry and farmers. This means some rivers have run dry, and the water table has fallen.

In many areas there has been a hosepipe ban, and restrictions on the use of water.

No place on earth gets the same amount of rain every year, and scientists are always thinking of ways to make more water. 'Seeding' clouds is one way. Planes fly over clouds and dump chemicals in them to produce more rain. Taking the salt out of sea water is another way. And scientists have even looked into towing icebergs to places that need more fresh water. But these expensive procedures probably wouldn't be necessary if we took better care of our water. And that means recycling it and keeping it clean.

Industrial Yuck

No matter what product they're making, factories end up with leftovers—chemicals, waste water, bits and pieces of this and that. When industries began many years ago, they found that the easiest place to dump their leftovers was in the water. After all, it just floats away . . . or does it?

Many industries used to dump their chemical waste directly into nearby rivers, lakes, and oceans. But soon fish started dying and people got sick from eating the fish and drinking the water.

People discovered they had to find a safer way to dispose of their wastes. Some companies started storing their wastes underground. But then chemicals leaked into the groundwater. Other industries built their own lakes to store their wastes. But as the lake water evaporated, it left the chemicals behind. These chemicals became more and more concentrated and eventually seeped into the groundwater.

But a lot of industries are finding safe and healthy ways of disposing of their chemical wastes. In Europe, ships with incinerators carry the wastes far out to sea and burn them. The burning chemicals create dangerous gases that mix with the air. But by the time the gases reach cities and towns, they are harmless. Some waste, such as radioactive waste from nuclear power plants, cannot be burned. But it can be sealed up in glass or pottery containers and buried with no danger of leaking.

Do You Know What You're Drinking?

There have been a number of Acts of Parliament to make sure that the water companies process water which meets certain standards. There are also EC directives on the quality of water in our taps, and its safety.

Much of our drinking water comes from the ground. Dangerous chemicals can get into groundwater, and they don't always come from factories. How many different bottles and cans of cleaning solution do you have in your house? What happens to the bottles and cans when they are empty? Probably you throw them in the dustbin, like everyone else.

Most cities and towns send their garbage to landfills. In a landfill, the rubbish is dumped and covered over with soil. Eventually much of it breaks down and mixes with the soil. But plastic cleaner bottles and spray cans don't. And the little drops of chemicals left in them can leak out. If the landfill is badly made, rain washes these chemicals into the soil. The chemicals seep into the underground aquifers and contaminate the water supply for people who have wells.

Even chemicals we use for good reasons can pollute our drinking water. Farmers spray pesticides on their crops to protect them from insects. But these pesticides can seep into the groundwater and contaminate aquifers as well as nearby streams and ponds. The same thing happens with weed killers and other chemicals people spray on their lawns.

Groundwater pollution is dangerous not only for people, but for all living things. Plants and trees absorb water from the ground into their stems and leaves. If the water contains harmful chemicals, plants and trees will suffer.

Acid Rain, Go Away

The purest water in the world is contained in clouds. In areas with little pollution, rain and snow falls to the ground with very few impurities in it. But when the air is polluted, the raindrops pick up chemicals on the way down. This is called acid rain. Cars and factories put nitrous oxide and sulphur into the air. Most nitrous oxide comes from the fuel used by cars. Sulphur comes from burning coal, now mainly used by power stations to make electricity. When these chemicals mix with water, they form acids.

Acids of one kind or another are all around us. Some, such as lemon juice and orange juice, are citric acids that are naturally found in food. Vinegar is an acid too. But nitric acid and sulphuric acid are much more

TRY IT!
Cut a stalk of celery with leaves on it and put it in a glass of water. Mix in two drops of blue or red food colouring and a tablespoon of household cleaner. Check the celery every hour or so. You'll see the coloured water being drawn up to the leaves. How long before the leaves begin to wilt and die from the cleaning chemicals?

DID YOU KNOW?

Lead is another dangerous water contaminant. Lead can get into anybody's water, no matter where you live, because it doesn't come from the ground. It comes from old water pipes. Plumbers sometimes use lead to solder together pipes in houses. If the pipes and solder are old or damaged, lead can flake off from the solder and mix with the water that flows through the pipes. Lead poisoning can make people very sick. If you live in an old house, you may want to have your water tested for lead.

dangerous. In the eastern part of North America, for example, acid rain has poisoned many lakes so much that nothing can live in them. If you live in an area like that, it's probably not a good idea to try catching snowflakes on your tongue!

Many people are trying to clean up the air and reduce acid rain. In some places, laws forbid new factories from releasing sulphur into the air. And oil companies around the world are constantly working to produce petrol products that are less harmful to the environment. But the world still has a long way to go in reducing acid rain.

Oil and Water Don't Mix

TRY IT!

What happens to water when oil gets in it? Fill a clear glass with water and slowly pour in one-half cup of cooking oil. Watch through the side of the glass while you're pouring. Where does the oil go? Imagine the same thing happening with crude oil spilling into the ocean from an oil well or an oil tanker, a huge ship carrying millions of gallons of oil.

On 24 March, 1989, an oil tanker owned by the Exxon company crashed and spilled fifty million litres of crude oil into Prince William Sound, off the coast of Valdez, Alaska. Exxon workers first tried to keep the spill in the ocean so it

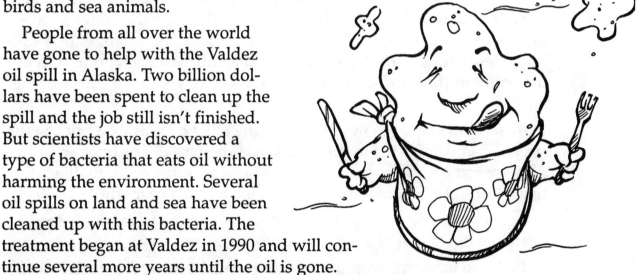

wouldn't wash up on the beach. When that didn't work, they had to start wiping it up with towels. Try wiping up two or three tablespoons of cooking oil with a paper towel. Now multiply that mess by fifty million litres! As a result of that one spill, thousands of fish, geese, sea otters, and other wildlife were killed.

Every year thousands of oil spills occur. Many of them are small spills of less than 4,500 litres. But some, like the Exxon Valdez, are disastrous. In 1978 an oil tanker called the *Amoco Cadiz* ran aground near France and spilled over 300 million litres of oil into the Atlantic Ocean. Another spill in 1990 occurred when a Norwegian tanker exploded in the Gulf of Mexico. Fortunately, the oil caught fire before it could spread to the Texas coast. But the smoke and fumes from the fire killed many birds and sea animals.

People from all over the world have gone to help with the Valdez oil spill in Alaska. Two billion dollars have been spent to clean up the spill and the job still isn't finished. But scientists have discovered a type of bacteria that eats oil without harming the environment. Several oil spills on land and sea have been cleaned up with this bacteria. The treatment began at Valdez in 1990 and will continue several more years until the oil is gone.

Working Together

Many countries have laws that keep industries from wasting and polluting too much water. But for the rest of us, the only way to keep our water healthy and plentiful is for each person to play a part. Each drop of water that goes down the drain is important. It can stay around forever—if it gets cleaned and can be used again. Each person who uses water is important too. Unless we all use water responsibly, it might not be around when we need it. The next few pages will give you ideas on how you and your family can take better care of the water around you.

Waste Not, Want Not

Remember the water use log your family made in Chapter 6? Read through the log again and talk to your family. Where can you cut back on water use? Here are some suggestions:

1. When you can, take short showers instead of baths. Turn off the water while you're getting soapy. Then turn it back on to rinse.

2. The same goes for washing your hands and face and brushing your teeth. Turn the water on to wet and rinse only.

3. Check your house for leaky taps and pipes. Turn on the water at each sink and check the pipes underneath while the water's running. Are any dripping? You can check for leaks in the toilet by putting a few drops of food colouring in the tank. After an hour, check the water in the bowl. Is it coloured too? If so, you have a leak in the tank.

4. You can save even more water in the toilet by putting a brick in the tank. When you flush, the tank fills to a certain level. The brick will displace some water so the tank won't need as much water to fill it. But there will still be enough water in the tank to flush properly.

5. Don't run the cold water until it's cold enough to drink. Keep a container of water in the refrigerator for drinking.

6. Avoid using the washing machine or dishwasher for small loads, unless it has a half-load button.

7. Take another look at how much water your family uses in the garden. Grass needs only three centimetres of water a week to stay healthy. If it rains once a week, you don't need to water at all. When you do water, put a container under the sprinkler spray. When it fills to three centimetres, turn the water off.

8. If you live in an area with little rainfall, in the east of Great Britain, look into building a drought garden. Ask at your local garden centre, or visit the one at Rutland Water for ideas.

Keep It Clean!

The cleaner you keep the water around you, the more water you'll have to use over and over again. And when the water's healthy, plants, trees, animals, and you will be healthier too. Here are some ways your family can help keep the groundwater clean in your area. And some ideas for recycling household waste.

1. Be careful about what you throw away. Don't pour oil, paint, or other chemicals into storm sewers or down the drain. Find out if your town has a toxic-waste collection system that will pick up used paint cans and empty chemical containers. Many larger petrol stations now recycle used oil.

2. Recycle and re-use as many containers as you can. Try to buy products that come in recyclable containers, such as cardboard, glass, aluminum, and steel. If you must buy something that comes in plastic, try to think of another use for the plastic container when it's empty. The less rubbish in landfills, the better off our groundwater will be.

3. Start a compost heap to recycle your food scraps and lawn clippings. Wrap chicken wire around four posts to make a box. Layer in grass clippings, weeds, leaves, and kitchen scraps—anything except meat and fish. Keep the compost material damp and turn it occasionally. By next summer you'll have organic fertilizer for your lawn and garden.

4. Try to use lawn and garden products that don't contain harmful chemicals. Organic fertilizers and weed killers use special bacteria and nutrients to do the job rather than harmful chemicals.

5. Use the family car as little as possible to cut back on acid rain. Ride bikes, walk, or take the bus or train whenever you can.

Be a Water Watchdog!

You can make a difference in our world's water just by keeping your eyes open!

IN THE PARK . . .

pick up and throw away any litter you see in ponds and puddles. Check the colour of the water in the ponds and streams. Is it green or very muddy? Is it a funny orange or red colour? Does it have soap suds in it? If so, report this to the Parks Department in your local council offices so they can clean it up.

AT THE BEACH . . .

take along a rubbish bag and pick up anything that you see on the beach and in the shallow water. Especially look for old fishing line. Birds and other creatures can get tangled up in it. Whatever you take to the beach with you, be sure you either throw it in a rubbish bin or bring it back home with you.

WHEN YOU'RE CAMPING . . .

take your own drinking water. Don't wash your dishes or yourself in the lake or stream unless you have biodegradable soap. Use the campsite's toilets if there are any. If not, dig a hole in the ground to use as a toilet. But be sure it's well away from any streams or ponds. When you leave, bring everything back home with you. Try to make the campsite look as if nobody had even been there.

AT SCHOOL . . .

talk to your teacher about how your class can conserve water and keep it clean. You could check the building for leaky taps, pipes, and toilets. Put signs in the cloakrooms encouraging others not to let the water run while they're washing their hands. Ask the caretaker to put bricks in the toilet tanks. How many other ideas can you think of?

Conclusion

Water is the most important and the most plentiful substance in the world. God created everything on earth to live and work and grow together. All living things depend on water to keep them healthy and alive. And water depends on people to take care of it and use it wisely. No matter where or how water appears—across the street or on the other side of the world, in the sky or under the ground—let's keep it flowing clean and strong. When we all work together, we can make sure that our water can keep doing its job for many years to come. And we can continue to enjoy the oceans, lakes, ponds, and puddles that help to make our world a wonderful place to live.

Notes

Notes

Notes

Notes

Notes

Notes

Notes

Notes

Notes